Photo Fabrications

Easy machine appliqué from family photos

by

Angela Madden

Acknowledgments.

To Jeremy Froy of J. I. Froy Computer Consultancy Barton-le-Clay, Beds. for responding so helpfully to my anguished cries .....
(and there were several !!) ...... for help with the new computer and digital camera.

Sue Martin, Jane Plowman, and Martin Mc Donald for technical assistance.

Margaret Bright, Nora Field, Jenny Hipperson, Alison King,
Sue Martin, Jane Plowman, Carmen Redler, Mary Rich,
Davina Thomas, Josie Warrington, and Shirley Winchester, who agreed to be my 'guinea pigs' and following a workshop, kindly lent their work to be photographed.

C. June Barnes
and Katherine Letherby of 'Moor Silks and Quilts', Tavistock, Devon. for lending photographs.

ISBN 0 952 1060 7 8
First edition 1999.

M.C.Q. Publications.
19, Barlings Rd.
Harpenden, Herts.
AL5 2AL.
England.

Distributor in U.S.A.
Quilters' Resource Inc.
P.O. Box 148850.
Chicago. Illinois 60614.
U.S.A.

Distributor in New Zealand.
Margaret Barrett Distributors
19, Beasley Ave.
P.O. Box 12 - 034.
Penrose. Auckland.
New Zealand.

Table of contents.

Introduction.

Yes ... all the coloured photographs in this book are of quilts ....
i.e. made of appliquéd fabric, not painted. Most are the end result of someone willing to try their hand at this technique for the first time. The sewers involved are not artists ... few would describe themselves as 'artistic'. Their common link was that they were willing to have a try at something which was new to them ... and by doing so they have opened up a new and exciting possibility in their quiltmaking repertoire ... the inclusion of great pictures.

It is a wonderful gift, possessed by a lucky few, which enables them to draw or paint a good likeness. The goal of the techniques described in the following pages is to enable many more than the lucky few to reproduce 'a good likeness' by copying a photograph in fabric.

Copying from a photograph ......
is not a negative second class type of artistic activity.
It is not creating a forgery or fake of the 'real thing'.
It is a great way of enabling us all to stretch our abilities,
increase our knowledge ..... sharpen our observation
and achieve what would otherwise prove impossible.

Photographs of almost anything can be copied for appliqué .....
friends and family ..... trees and landscapes ... animals ... cars, planes and trains ... flowers and fruit ... alphabets ... buildings ... fish and underwater scenes ... birds ... statues and stonework ... old masters ... celebrities ... wedding and fashion pictures ... sports figures ... insects ... and fungi .... whatever !

Small children enthusiastically tackle the above subjects with crayons, paint and pencils. They have fun! They do not yet know that they are unable to do this because they are 'not artistic'. Learning that we are 'not artistic' is for many the only legacy of school art lessons. This label later prevents us from trying to do something we might otherwise attempt.
'Arty things' are O.K. for others ... but not for us.

What if we were just going about it in the wrong way ... like trying to play the piano with our toes .... or reading books upside down?
What if we never found out we could do it by another method ... because we never gave it a try?
The main requirement of this technique is the ability to look closely at photographs .... and draw around what you see. The rest if easy.

Surprise yourself ... and have fun along the way!!

Supplies

These are the supplies that we need to create a 'Photo Fabrication'.........
An explanation of each follows.

Acetate.
Carbon paper.
Camera, (optional).
Cotton batting / wadding.
Fabrics ...100% cotton.
Fabric covered board, (optional).
Freezer paper.
Fusible web.
Fusible mending/binding tape.
Fine point, coloured permanent marking pens.
Lead mechanical pencil.
Machine needles ... sizes 60, 80 and 'Metallica'.
Machine feet.
Non-stick ironing sheet.
Overhead projector pen.
Photographs.
Photocopy ... (enlarged) of photograph.
Scissors.
Spray starch.
Threads.

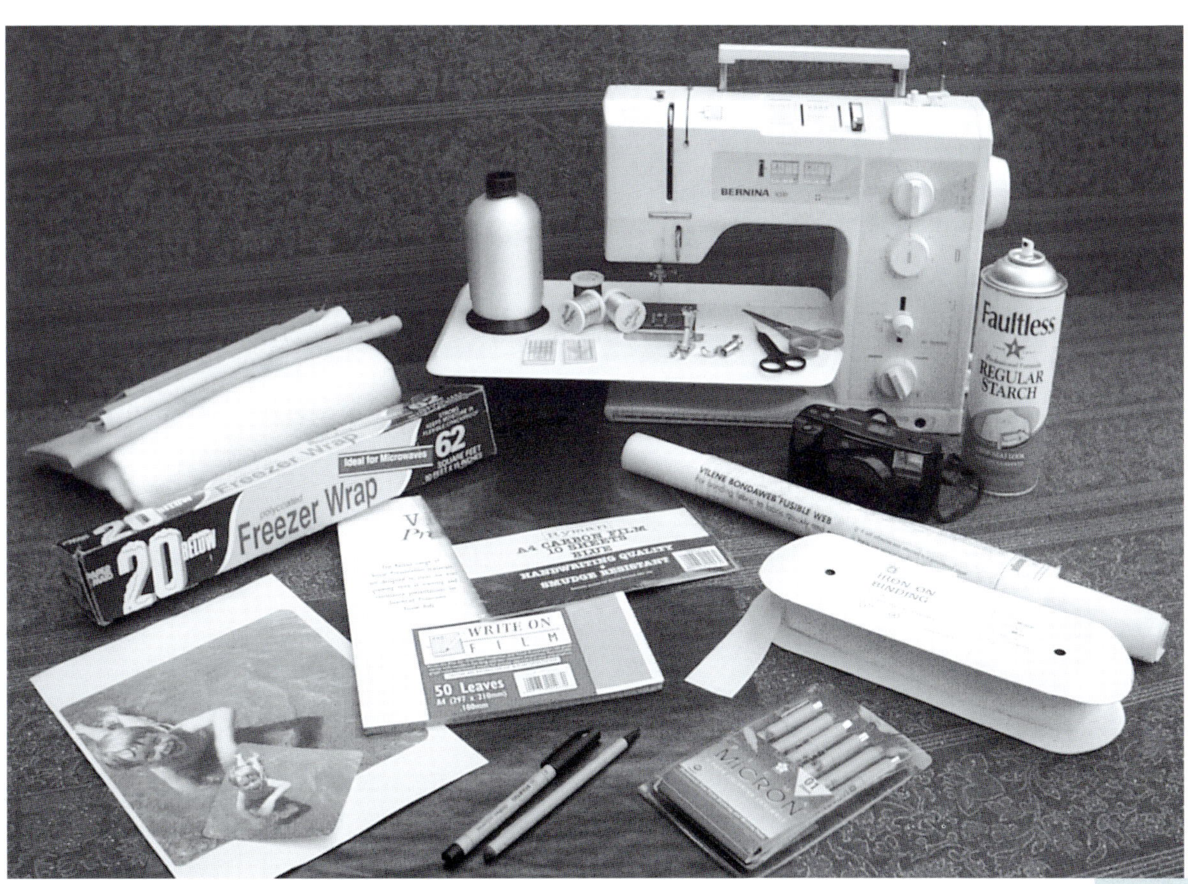

Supplies explained.

Here are some general points about the items that we will need to use for this technique. When using the right tools and equipment things are more likely to go well, and a task can be a pleasure .... while the opposite, unfortunately, is also true.

Acetate.

Sheets of acetate are used in addition to carbon paper to help identify and mark design lines from the colour photocopy of your photograph. Such sheets are readily available from office supply, or art shops in boxes or tear off pads. Some are designed as overhead projector transparencies. It is not necessary to buy the quality necessary to pass ***through*** a photocopier. Photocopying onto acetate is not a requirement for this technique.

Carbon paper.

This is the principal aid used to make a working design which will create our appliqué pattern. Packets are readily available from office supply shops and stationers. It is essential to use smudge free, handwriting quality and not typewriting quality.
A sheet of carbon placed between a photocopy and a blank sheet of paper enables lines drawn on the photocopy to be accurately transferred to the blank sheet.
The main advantage of using carbon paper over tracing paper is that you always have a completely clear view of the item that you wish to reproduce.
I always feel that tracing details from a photograph through tracing paper requires amazing eyesight and a lot of guesswork. It can be like peering through a fog and often requires frequent checks with the original for reassurance.

Camera.

This is only required if you wish to take photographs to use for this technique. It is not necessary to have a top of the range camera. Any good compact camera will be fine.

Cotton batting / wadding.

I like to use cotton batting. Frequently I use it in a double layer when making wallhangings as the extra layer adds weight, and I feel that they look better when hung. The extra layer also adds loft to the portraits in contrast to the background which looks good when flattened by heavy quilting.

Fabrics.

100% cotton fabrics work best, but other fabrics can be used if they are firmly woven and are not inclined to fray. Nylon backed metallics can add sparkle ... especially to appliqué frames.

Conventional quilting wisdom recommends pre-washing all fabrics. I prefer to test fabrics for shrinkage or unstable dye by putting a small measured square of each into a white bowl of hot water. Bleeding colour will show up against the white, and the square can be measured for shrinkage after drying. Only those fabrics which demonstrate problems need to be washed.

The number, yardage and colour of fabrics that will be required will depend upon the project undertaken. However, individual fabrics are usually needed in very small quantities.

A fabric covered board.

This is an optional, but useful item. I prefer to assemble the appliqué on top of a fabric covered board. When fusing the edges of fabric shapes together, this provides a firmer surface than my ironing board to press against. It has the added advantage of making my work portable should I want to move it. I can store the board leaving everything in place on top, and it will be ready to go when I want to continue.

A piece of covered softboard is ideal as I can pin into it, anchoring any wayward pieces of paper or fabric that might go A.W.O.L.

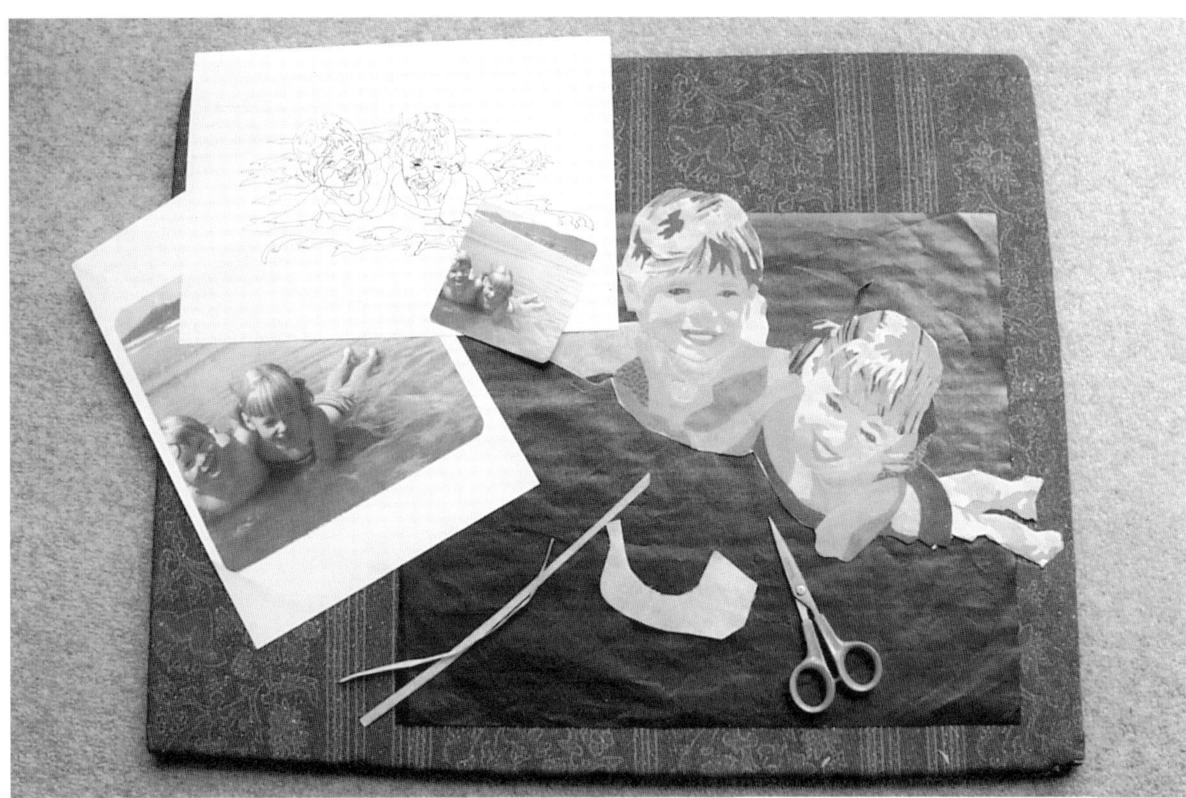

Freezer paper.

If you are unfamiliar with this type of paper ... it is useful because it sticks to fabric when ironed with the shiny side against it, but is easily removed, leaving no residue. Designs can be drafted on the dull side. It is therefore ideal for making templates and is consequently a great quilter's aid.

It is available by the roll in the U.S.A. as a food wrap and also from most quilt shops worldwide. Although at first glance it does not look like a tracing paper, it is quite possible to use it as such, provided the design lines are sufficiently clear and dark enough to show through.

Substitute papers such as the outer wrappers of photocopying paper are not suitable for the techniques in this book. Many carry printed advertising and are too thick and opaque to allow tracing.

I have recently discovered a great new free source; ..... it is used as packing between some brands of new aluminium printing plates used by lithographic printers. It is well worth checking out local printing firms and asking them to save it for you. Printers will not call it 'freezer paper' .... so a description of the dull and shiny side will probably be necessary.

Printer's paper is blank and is usually thinner than supermarket paper.
This makes tracing even easier.
It comes as a full sheet at 28 x 24 ins. / 72 x 61 cm. and also in half that size.
Both sizes are convenient for projects, or they can be taped together should larger sheets ever be needed.

(Always test that any clear tape used for joining freezer paper sheets will withstand the heat of an iron. In my experience different brands have different heat tolerances ... some tapes melt away completely, but it will not tell you that on the wrapper !).

Fine point, coloured permanent pens.

Pens such as Pigma™ Micron fine point pens are sold in quilt shops for marking fabric. They are used for making quilt labels and for other decorative purposes. They are permanent markers which are fade and water resistant, and are therefore ideal for adding details which are too small to be executed in appliqué.

Black and brown are the most useful colours .... great for such purposes as adding pupils and lashes to eyes .... blue can be useful for re-touching blue eyes.
The finer the pen point used, the better the final result. Shading effects can be added in a series of tiny dots which blend imperceptibly into the overall image.

Fusible web.

My fusible of choice for this technique is Bondaweb™. also known as Vliesoflex™. or Wonder Under,™. depending on where in the world it is sold. This very fine, fusible bonding web is paper backed and heat activated. Readily available from shops selling dressmaking and quilting supplies, it is sold in packets or by the metre from a roll.

Ironing the web through the paper onto fabric will fuse the web to the fabric. The paper prevents the fusible sticking to and gumming up the iron and can then be peeled away and discarded. If the fused side of the fabric is placed on top of a second fabric, once again, when ironed they will fuse together. The bond will be firm enough to hold the two fabric layers together .... but is not permanent and they can be pulled apart to separate.

There are several similar fusible products available. To date I have not found another that works better than Bondaweb™ for this technique. Some brands are too heat sensitive .... i.e. they lose their ability to adhere if the iron temperature exceeds a silk setting. Others provide a completely permanent bond ... ideal for some purposes, but not for this. The ability to unstick and dismantle a fused portion of work provides a valuable 'safety net' should you make a mistake .... (well who is infallible ?) .. and flexibility if you change your mind over a colour choice.

For this technique I recommend that Bondaweb™. is bought from the roll, in no more than half metre lengths, and wrapped around a cardboard tube taken to the shop for the purpose of safeguarding it during the journey home.

Allowing the web to be folded and put into a bag causes the bond between the fusible and the paper to weaken. If this happens the two layers can separate before it is used, making it difficult to handle. This can also occur with pre-packed or old Bondaweb ™. (Do not worry ... there is an easy cure on page 55).

Unless the web and the paper remain united they can be difficult to manage. This is particularly crucial for this technique since we will be cutting the fusible into very narrow strips. These strips will be fused around the the outer edges of fabric shapes so that they can be bonded together. The interior of each appliqué shape will not be fused.

When any two fabrics are bonded together they stiffen and feel more rigid as a result. Appliqués which have been totally fused to the backing fabric can feel a little hard to the touch. The lovely soft undulations which make quilting so attractive are usually lost because the added stiffness flattens the surface of the work.

The use of fusible strips for this technique enables fabric layers to be anchored in position until the stitching is completed which will hold the fabrics permanently. It is the vital ingredient which makes the technique speedy and easy .... but is undetectable in the finished work.

Fusible mending / binding tape.

This tape is sold by the metre in haberdashery shops for binding and mending purposes. It is available in different colours ... (but we only require white) .. with a shiny fusible side which adheres to fabric when ironed. It is 1 1/2in. .. 38 mm. wide. I find white fusible mending tape wonderful for placing the reflected pinpoints of light in eyes, so only a tiny amount is required in any project.

Lead mechanical pencil.

The supermarket variety is ideal. Such pencils have fine leads which maintain a uniform thickness throughout the work. They also usually have an eraser !

Non-stick ironing sheet.

This is a fabric sheet which has been impregnated with Teflon™ to prevent anything sticking to it. It is an ***essential*** item for this technique, and generally useful when using fusibles of any kind, being a great help throughout the assembly process. Both iron and ironing board can be protected from sticking to stray fusible web. These sheets are available from quilts shops and also from many grocery stores, where they are called non stick 'cooking' sheets. The colour, size and price may vary, but essentially they are identical.

Overhead projector pen.

These fibre tipped pens will write on acetate while ordinary pens will not. Available from office supply shops they are sold in various colours and different widths. The type that you require is ...

fine tipped ..... black ... and .... non - permanent.

The ability to erase lines ..... ('cotton wool buds' and tissues are used for this) is valuable in case of error and also enables the acetate sheets to be re-used many times.

Photographs.

These are the starting point for our 'Photo Fabrications'. Any of your favourite family snapshots can be considered for use ...... check out the album now !

Photocopies.

As most photographs are too small for details to be conveniently traced, it is necessary to enlarge them by colour photocopying or computer scanning.

Sewing machine.

Any model which has a 'swing needle' facility and can therefore sew a zig-zag stitch is suitable.

Sewing machine needles.

Size 60 needles are fine, specialist needles which punch very small holes making joins stitched with invisible thread barely visible. They are brittle needles and can be easily broken, so they are not suitable for general sewing purposes. However, if used selectively, they are worth the investment and are ideal for sewing the nearly invisible joins in these projects.
Metallica needles are the choice for sewing metallic decorative threads.
Size 80 needles are good utility needles for sewing on borders and for other similar tasks.

Sewing machine feet.

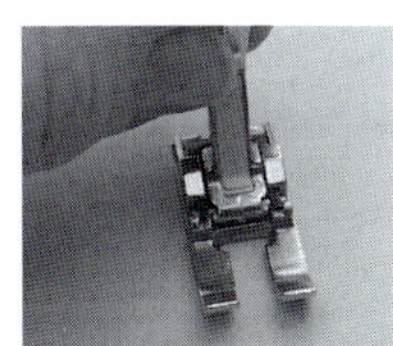

An open toe embroidery foot is a vital sewing machine accessory which enables the sewer to have an unrestricted view of the area immediately in front of the needle. They are seldom included in the kit which comes with a new machine but can be bought separately and are useful for many more purposes than embroidery.

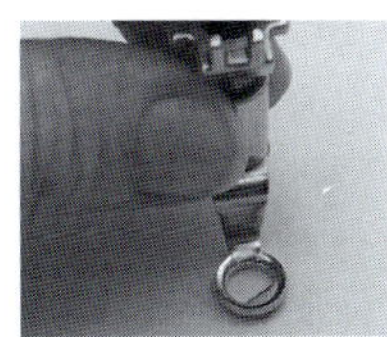

A darning, (or quilting, or free embroidery) foot is necessary to accomplish the quilting around irregular shapes as it allows the fabric to move freely in any direction during stitching. (One may be included in the basic machine kit).

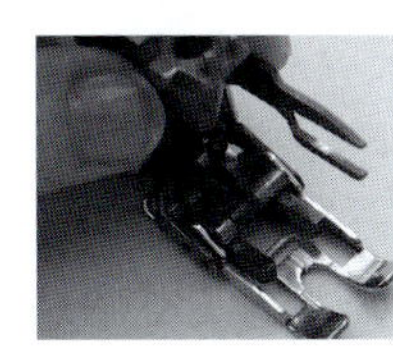

A walking / even feed foot advances both the top and bottom fabric layers of the quilt at the same rate and so enables straight lines and large curves to be quilted without producing wrinkles on the back of the quilt. (Once again this foot is not usually included in the basic machine kit).

Scissors.

It is very important to use small sharp scissors which cut efficiently right up to and including the extreme tip of the blades. Whether these scissors have curved or straight blades is a matter of personal preference.
Accurate fine cutting will definitely not be possible with large handled or blunt scissors .... so it is worth investing in a suitable pair before you start ...... to save frustration once your project is underway.

Spray starch.

The application of starch to fabric can temporarily stiffen it, making it behave more like paper, and therefore making it easier to cut, sew and handle. Always spray the fabric lightly on the wrong side in case the heat of the iron makes it shiny. Starching is especially helpful if fabric has been pre-washed and become floppy, giving it back that 'new' appearance and feel. I like to apply starch to fabric before I cut into it ... and at frequent intervals during assembly.

Threads.

Nylon monofilament thread is used for sewing the fabric sections together. This 'invisible thread' is less noticeable than matching thread, creating a lighter join and adding no extra colour or bulk. Two colours are available ......
'clear' for light coloured fabrics and 'smoke' for dark.
Always use a good quality named brand ... many unbranded threads are more suitable for fishing line than sewing.

Match the bobbin thread to the fabric colour. Do not put invisible thread in the bobbin.
Metallic or coloured embroidery threads can be used for decorative purposes in backgrounds and on frames.

Above, a magnified seam sewn with nylon thread using an open zig-zag stitch.

Above, a magnified seam sewn with matching colour thread. The right half has been sewn with satin stitch and the left half with the same open zig-zag as above.
In both these alternatives the stitching line is heavier and more noticeable.

The 'Photo Fabrication' process.

The individual stages in the process are ....

1. Choosing a photograph to copy.
2. Enlarging the image for tracing.
3. Tracing to create a working design.
4. Enlarging the working design to actual size.
6. Turning the design into freezer paper templates.
7. Choosing suitable fabrics.
8. Cutting fabric shapes.
9. Joining fabric shapes.
10. Sewing joins.
11. Removing freezer paper.
12. Adding detail.
13. Appliquéing the image to a background.
14. Adding an optional border .... or designing a frame.
15. Quilting the image.
16. Making a quilt label.

None of these stages is difficult ....

and a detailed explanation of each follows ....

Choosing a Photograph to copy.

Regardless of whether you can draw or not, using a photograph as a starting point for stitching a life-like image makes good sense. You can choose an existing favourite or set out to snap another to suit. Either way you will have an image which can be copied. This can help you achieve a good likeness.
The technique described will concentrate on reproducing faces, but the same principles apply to all images.
Everyone responds to a good likeness of someone they know, be it in paint, on film or even in fabric. Such replicas contain a touch of magic. It is no wonder that primitive people felt that taking their photograph captured their soul. We all treasure images of people, places, animals and things which have significance to us. We carry them about in wallets and pockets ... pin them up, frame them on walls, send them to each other ... and many would give priority to saving their favourites in the event of a fire!
Such images provide emotional bridges during separation, either temporary or permanent. They are ways of recording important events .... moments locked in time ..... as memories and mementos.
When a photograph is taken ..... the scene and moment are no longer lost in the past.

All of the above can be true of quilted pictures too ... and in addition ...... quilts are tactile, three dimensional .... and quilters enjoy making them !!

Many of us will already have photographs that we would like to reproduce in fabric. When looking through your collection for something suitable, bear the following in mind ......

1. Your family photos do not need to be of art gallery standard for this technique. It is a misconception that you can only use really fabulous photos ..... snapshots are fine.

2. The image you choose must be clear enough, when enlarged, to see well defined features.

3. You can be selective in what you use from less than perfect photos ...
if the subject is off centre ...... he/she can be correctly placed in the appliqué.
If he/she has a tree growing out of their head ... it can be omitted.
You can put the head from one photo on the body of another ....
As the designer, you can make changes which will improve any subject and make it work.

4. If you choose a photo that you like, you will enjoy making and seeing the result.
There are no 'hard' or 'easy' photos .... only ones that will take more time to complete as they contain more and perhaps smaller detail.

Taking suitable photographs.

If you feel the need or desire to take new photographs, here are some suggestions:

Whether indoors or out, find a suitable location to get the best from your subject, somewhere they will feel at ease and will not be embarrassed or distracted by an audience. Taking several photos in quick succession .... perhaps when they do not expect it, may produce a winner.

Do your best to help them to relax .... so that they will not look 'posed'.
If they are too self-conscious the result will be un-natural.

Try positions other than being square on to the camera .... suggest turning sideways and relaxing the shoulders.

Distract children with a toy ..... or someone to watch off camera, or take shots when they are interested in something and not expecting it.

Silly photos, or shots which may cause later embarrassment, are best avoided ...... even if they were funny at the time!

Position feet and legs carefully if they are to be included. Limbs snapped in odd positions can result in the subject appearing deformed.

Asymmetrical poses are more interesting .... e.g. one side passive, the arm relaxed, the hand closed ... one side active ... the arm raised and the hand open.

Requesting that your model wears light or medium coloured clothes will enable more interesting shadows to be seen than if they are dressed in dark colours.

Do not get too close to the subject as this can cause size distortions.
Use the telephoto setting if you have the option ...... and not the wide angle.

Only photograph the part that you intend to appliqué ... there is no point in taking a full figure shot if you only want the face.

Whilst outdoors, facing the subject towards bright light will most probably cause them to squint and spoil the portrait. The light will also effectively bleach all the interesting shadow shapes from the face.

The degree of cloud cover can dramatically affect outdoor shots, while the height of the sun in the sky will affect the angle of shadow cast by the facial features. Morning and evening light is softer and more flattering than mid-day.

Check that no unexpected shadows fall across the subject's face from neighbouring trees or buildings etc. .... they will cause confusion when tracing.

If you choose to use additional lighting, check the degree and placement of any shadows which are cast. Careless lighting can increase the apparent size of facial characteristics such as the nose. Lighting from one side generally creates better shadow shapes than light from either above or below.

The colour of photos can also be dramatically affected by the light prevailing at the time they are taken ..... artificial light can create a yellowish tinge. Colour in the finished shots can be altered by the developer. If you are unhappy with the first result, have a discussion to see if it is worth having them developed once again with a different colour balance.
However, do not forget that you can ignore the photo colour altogether when choosing the fabric for the appliqué, so unless you want to match it *exactly* ... it is really not important.

Tip !

If you wish to include more than one portrait in the same project ....
but are unable to shoot them in the same photo ... thus perhaps requiring photography on different occasions .... it is important to match the direction of the light source in each shot.
Attention to this will enable you to combine photos from different times and settings.

A simple home made device ....
of a marked card with a pin pierced through it ...(rather like a sun dial) ..... placed on top of your camera will help identify the exact direction of the cast shadow before you take the photo.

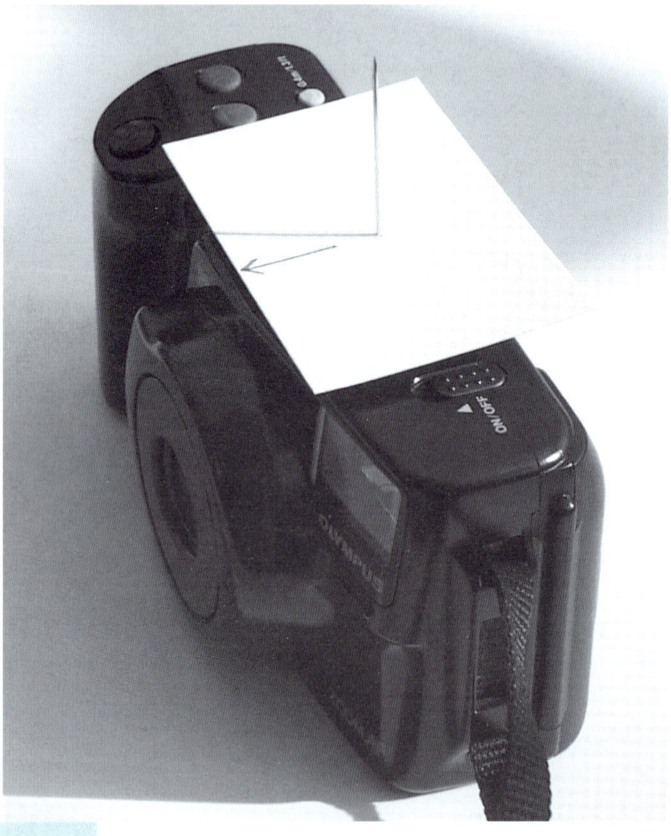

(the arrow points to the direction of the camera lens).

On each occasion mark and record the shadow direction cast by the pin on a card so it can be accurately duplicated. If you use existing photos you can guess the direction of the light and by using the pin and card device try to reproduce it as faithfully as possible. This will certainly be more accurate than taking pot luck.

(I always study the shadow cast by the nose and those in the fabric folds of clothing for light direction clues.)

Enlarging the image for tracing.

Photocopying machines have revolutionised life for both the artistic and the non-artistic alike. The time saved by copying or enlarging images for relatively little cost is immense.

The technique described in this book requires a clear, usually enlarged photocopy of your original photograph. The modern machines found in copy shops are ideal for this.

It is vital to have this photocopy done on a *colour* copy machine ....
.... **not a black and white machine.**

This rule applies regardless of whether your actual photograph has been taken in black and white, sepia or full colour.

Colour copying will not convert a black and white photo into colour .... but it will create a high definition image.

The colour copying process will cost a little extra ...... but is well worth it. The result will provide an infinitely better, more detailed image. In the hands of an experienced machine operator this process can be used to improve the quality of a less than perfect photo by lightening or darkening, and sharpening the image.

Colour changes can also be requested. Natural colour can be converted to sepia tones .... or corrections can be made to photographs that are deteriorating through the yellowing of ageing ....
or that were never the right colour in the first place.

If you choose to appliqué something which only occupies a small part of the total photo, do not feel that you have to enlarge the whole photo to enormous proportions to make that small part a suitable size to use. Parts of photos can be selectively copied without damage to the original .... leaving out what is not required.
A photocopy can also be taken from a slide. Many photocopy shops have the necessary special equipment and the cost is usually the same as for a photograph.

British paper size A4 .... (the size of a page in this book) or similar is a convenient size to make an enlargement ready for tracing. Double this is a good wallhanging size for an appliqué, especially with an added border.
Computer scanners can also manipulate and resize images..
Use a straightforward scan to obtain an identical copy of the the photo.
Splitting the image into different coloured areas and other 'fancy tricks' can cause unnecessary confusion.

Copyright.

It is necessary at this point to include a warning about copyright. Legally it is not possible to copy images by any means, if we do not own the copyright ourselves or have not obtained permission from the person who does.
A request for written permission to use someone else's material may incur a cost, if permission is granted. This may be substantial.

Many people are guilty of ignoring copyright. They photocopy, or trace designs and patterns from books, periodicals, cards, wrapping paper, fabric etc., without a thought for the fact that they are actually breaking the law and are, in theory, liable to prosecution.

It is often said that if a design is slightly altered, the copyright is cancelled and a new design has been created. This is not so ....

if the original design is ***substantially*** the same ....

The copyright law still applies.

While in the real world it is unlikely that a prosecution will follow if a copied photograph is used solely for personal purposes, it could be a different matter if the result were to be entered for exhibition or included in magazines or promotional material .... where the person who copied can be said to have profited from them.

The copyright of a photograph taken by someone other than yourself remains with the owner of the film. Therefore the use of professionally taken special occasion photographs such as graduation, wedding or celebrity pictures need permission to be granted for their reproduction. It is for this reason that reputable photocopy shops will refuse to duplicate any material they have concerns about. They will understandably be reluctant to run the risk of prosecution on your behalf.

If you are considering reproducing anything from a book, check the copyright statement which is usually included at the front. If in doubt ....
either request permission, or change your plans.

It is for this reason that I choose to concentrate on photographs that I have taken myself specially for a project .... family snapshots, ...
or vintage photographs over seventy years old and out of copyright.

This has the added advantages that the images I reproduce are guaranteed original .... are very personal, trouble free, and I can do with them whatever I wish.
In the related case of the exhibition of a project which is not a direct copy, but has been inspired by the work of another person, good practice requires that the original source be given credit.

Taking a closer look.

The painter Edouard Manet once observed....

"There are no lines in Nature ......

... only areas of colour ... one against another"

This is great news for patchworkers. Each area of colour is a shape. Each shape can be recreated in fabric as long as it forms an 'island' with an unbroken outline. To recreate a face from a photograph, in fabric, we need to trace the outline of all the shape islands and use the tracing as a design plan.
Magazine photos are a really good place to practice tracing outlines since they are readily available and disposable. Find several, as large as possible to start with, and study them closely. It can be difficult to identify features as islands if they are small or unclear.

Time needs to be spent analysing exactly what it is that we are seeing in our photograph. Notice that individual features often bear no resemblance to the common shorthand generalisations used when we draw faces from memory. The features are actually shapes containing light and dark colours.

Light affects everything that we see. The form of an object is made identifiable by the light that strikes some part of it and the shadow where the light does not reach. As needleworkers using fabric as our medium, we cannot replicate the detailed effects of light to the same extent as artists using paint. Nevertheless the correct use of colour to depict light and shadow in appliqué will give form to the images we create.

The lightness, or darkness, of a colour is called its 'tone'. It becomes easier to identify and evaluate tones if they are thought of as a scale of different coloured greys going from white through to black. We can easily see tones in a black and white picture, but 'darks' and 'lights' are also present in all other colours.

In the scale below each tone differs by 10% from its neighbours.

A black and white photograph may contain hundreds of different tones. We do not need to worry about this .. we can simplify our reproduction of the image by concentrating on the most important ones ...

the darkest 'darks' ... and ..... the lightest 'lights'......

these will define the main features of the image.

The addition of mid tones will create detail, interest and depth.
Choosing alternate tonal values on this scale will create contrast .... from a distance 'neighbours' can appear too similar.

When a single light source falls on a 3D object the effects are logical and unvaried. Simplifying the effect, we can see that they always create two clearly defined areas.

1. A bright side .... the area which faces the light ...... where we can see the lightest and brightest colours. What we actually see is a combination of the original colour of the item and the degree of light falling upon it.

2. A shadow side .... which may not be uniformly dark ..... as it may be collecting reflected light from neighbouring objects.

in addition we can usually see ....

a. Half tones .... areas which are tilted at slight angles to the main light source, causing slight colour variations.

b. Highlights .... usually the lightest lights and appear where a shiny, or reflective surface such as the end of the nose, the surface of the eye, or as in the example below, the skin of an apple, reflects back the original light source

c. Cast shadow .... these are the areas which can be seen on the ground or on neighbouring areas where the object itself blocks the light. Cast shadows echo the shape of the object ..... but may distort it ... e.g. elongate it ... according to the angle at which the light rays are travelling. Think of the length of winter or evening shadows compared with those seen at high noon. Cast shadows can have hard, clearly defined edges and are always attached to, or near to, the object blocking the light. They are usually darker than simple shadow, if they are not lightened by any reflected light.
However, cast shadows are never jet black ... except in comic books.

More than one light source may fall on a person or object, and they may come from different directions. Where this occurs multiple shadows will appear, causing confusion. For our purposes such pictures are best avoided.

Fabric colours correspond to a printed greyscale.

Taking a black and white photocopy of small pieces of fabric can provide a good visual guide to their comparitive tone.

Remember...
any colour fabric is only dark or light by comparison with its neighbour.

Choosing to put colours which are very close in both colour and tone as neighbours will make them visually run together when viewed from a distance.

Contrasts are vital to success.

The wrong side of many fabrics can be used to extend the colour range of your palette. It is usually a couple of tones lighter than the right side.

'Hi there !'

19 x 19 ins.
by
Sue Martin.

**Boxmoor,
Herts.**

'Still Life'
19 1/2 x 17ins
by

**Davina
Thomas.**

**St Albans,
Herts.**

Hard and soft edges.

Shapes can have either hard or soft edges. Examples of both can be seen in most photographs.

Hard edges have clearly defined borders ... e.g. a collar edge against a neck. These borders usually contrast sharply in tone with the next shape.

They occur mainly in the light-struck side of the face .... along bony ridges and sharp skin creases ... or between the figure and the background.
These edges are easy to trace and must be included.

Soft edges do not have such clearly defined borders ....
they gradually shade into the next colour.

They occur mostly on the shadow side of the face ..... and generally describe undulations .... e.g. in the hollow of the cheek and the curve of the forehead. These are more confusing to trace, and decisions have to be taken to include them or leave them out. A judgement must be made of how important they are to the overall image.

Artists can decide to fade one colour into another, very gradually blending them together as they paint. As fabric artists we cannot do this .... we either have one piece of fabric or another .... they have to be stitched together and cannot be blended .... even if they are similar in tone and colour there will always be a noticeable edge at the join between them.

We have to make a decision to include a shape or to ignore it.
If we include it .... it will have a hard edge. We must judge the consequences it will have on the image ... will it clarify and enhance it .... or merely form an unnecessary distraction ? Too many joins in a face can look like the subject has overdone the plastic surgery !

The mistake most likely to be made when learning to trace shapes is the inclusion of **every** shape that can be seen without being selective. Reproducing all of these with hard fabric edges can be very unflattering to the subject, causing them to become multi-coloured and craggy. It will also require lots of different fabrics to achieve such an undesirable look.

Practice tracing the following photos and compare your tracing with mine.
They will help you to make future tracing decisions.
However, do not feel that there is only one right decision.
There are choices .... and choices have effects.
Let 'what you personally like' be your guide. Experiment with alternatives.
The tracing **will** always look strange, and unconvincing .... it will be hard to convince yourself that it could ever be the basis for anything worthwhile.
Have Faith ! Shading shapes in pencil makes them look a little better ..... especially eyes. Page 41 explains the mechanics of tracing.

My Mother ...
Margaret Murphy..

You are invited to photocopy these photographs to practice tracing, then compare your finished tracings with mine over the page.
This head is a good size to copy .... tracing problems increase as size decreases.

' Lady.'

This photograph involves many more tracing decisions ...

where does the cat end and the cushion begin ?

which patterns on the cat's fur should be included ?

An enlargement will make these decisions easier.

Trace the clearest and most obvious features first.
Once again compare your tracing with mine overleaf ...you may prefer yours !
Always remember that if you are happy with a decision ... it's the right one.

'Lady'

Remember that the more shapes you include the more detailed and realistic the image becomes. It does not really become harder to complete ... it just takes longer to join more shapes.

When you look at a number of photos you will notice that there is considerable variation in the number of shadowed and highlighted areas ... i.e. shapes ..... that they contain. Some will contain a large number ..... others very few. Younger people's faces usually show few contrasts due to the roundness of their smooth skin which has few depressions, or wrinkles, to collect shadows. We 'earn' these as we gain years and 'character.'

Commercial photos will have been re-touched by artists to alter the appearance of the model. The usual purpose is to make them look more youthful ... especially if the photo is an advertisement for make up ..... or skin cream. Such photos may contain no shadow shapes, only eyes, nose and mouth ...... creating a bland image with few contrasts. Even so, you will see that the face is still a totally acceptable image. Some of your home photos may be similar. Look at the differences between the family photographs below ....

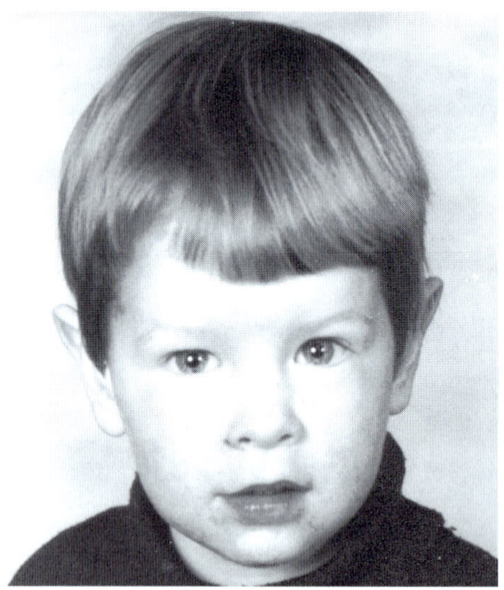

Son Rob aged four.

Daughter Laura as a teenager.

Brother-in-law Joe Madden.

My favourite Uncle .... John Moriarty.

Edouard Manet may be right stating that there are no *lines* in Nature .... only colours forming shapes. However, in photographs some shapes will always be narrow and *look like* thin lines. .... e.g. facial wrinkles or thin spectacle rims.

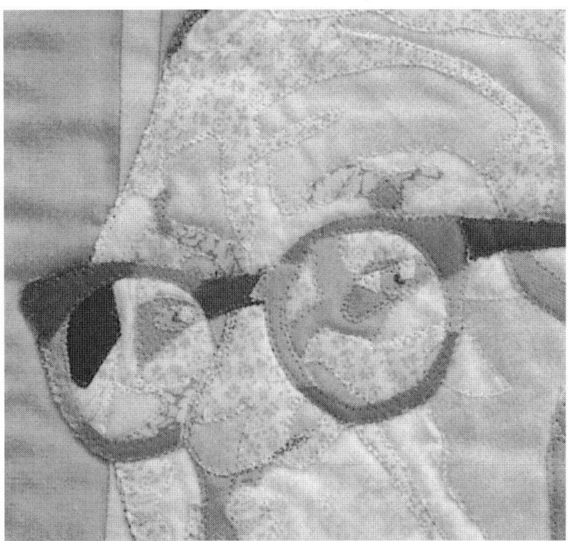

If we wish to include such a line in our appliqué we have to make a choice ...

1. **We can draw around it** .... turning it into a thin island.

2. **Or ..... trace it just as a line** .... remembering that as we cannot reproduce a very thin line in appliqué ...... it will have to be created by some other technique ... e.g. quilting ... machine embroidery or a drawn line ..... each of these alternatives would be added once the appliqué has been completed.

3. **Or .... ignore it** .... if we feel that it is not important to the image.

Used alone, the technique of appliqué has limitations for reproducing fine details. Lines are not the only thing we can choose to reproduce in another medium ..... jewellery ... hair ...... details on clothing etc. can enhance the 3D effect if we .... recreate them in embroidery .... or add them in beads .... lace, wool etc. If you wish to include skin wrinkles ... they can be added as quilting lines. The use of invisible thread will create the required depression without a coloured line which could look like a scar.

Tip !

Sometimes familiar characteristics can begin to look peculiar and unfamiliar when analysed in great detail. Turning your photocopy and looking at it upside down can help you to make a better tracing. It frees you from being governed by anticipated shapes. You can no longer recognise the upside down features, and you will be forced to examine what you see in a new and often much more accurate way.

Final decisions about the inclusion, or omission, of shapes in faces can be helped by thinking about the reasons that we apply cosmetics. If we apply light coloured eraser to dark shadows under eyes, or to hide skin discolouration, we can appear younger and healthier. 'Eye shadow' is applied to emphasise the eyes and blusher to contour the cheek bones.
These colours remove undesirable shadow shapes or form new ones to enhance appearance.
Likewise, the reason we apply compressed powder is to avoid greasy shine.
The purpose of careful studio lighting, as used for T.V. and film, is to flatter the subject, removing the ageing shadows without creating shine.
So why would we want to include **all** the shadows and shine in appliqué?

Sometimes both magazine and professionally taken photographs show heavy shadow to create drama.
A dark facial shadow may blend the face into a dark background without any visible division to show us where one ends and the other begins.
If you wish to copy such an image you have two choices.....

To merge ......
i.e. to reproduce the exact effect that we see .... making the facial shadow the same colour as the background .... ignoring the division that we know is really there.

or.

To guess .....
to draw a line which is a reasonable guess at where the division might possibly be and use a different colour on either side. The downside of guessing is that it will always introduce some degree of inaccuracy ... *but every single time that you trace a shape there is an element of guessing. It is the ability to guess that improves with practice.* Reproducing a photograph in another medium ... e.g. paint or fabric, inevitably introduces some element of change from the original .....
that's part of the charm ... but the essence of the photo remains. So, go on ... be brave ... guess !
I chose to guess the outline of the left side of my Grandfather's face when making the wallhanging on page 80.

Making eyes.

When examining photographs you will notice that eyes fall into three categories.

1. Solid coloured shapes containing no further detail. It is important to trace these shapes very accurately ..... they may not coincide with your memory of a symbol eye. These eyes contain no white.

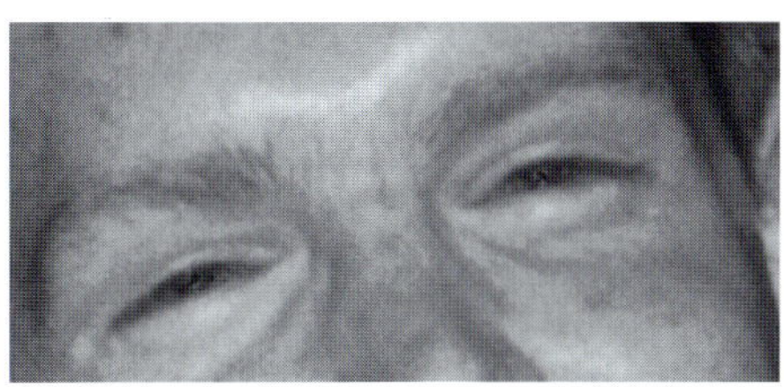 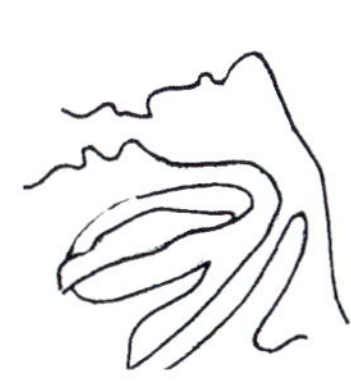  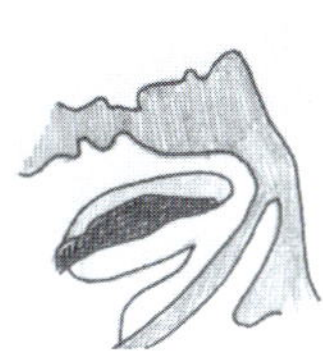 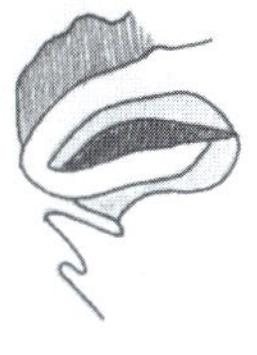

2. Semi-detailed eyes in which the white is visible but the pupil cannot be seen. These may or may not contain reflected light. These are often brown eyes.

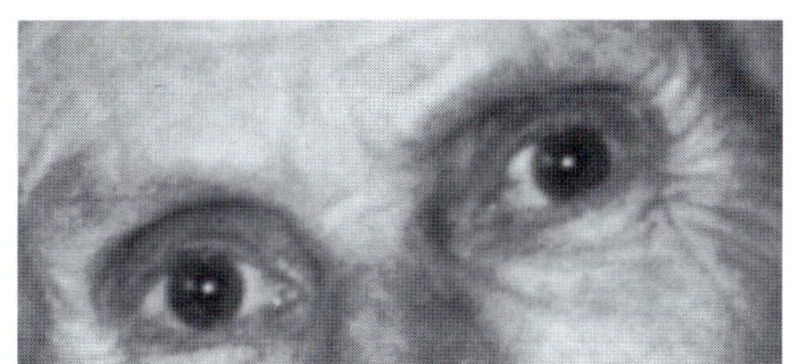 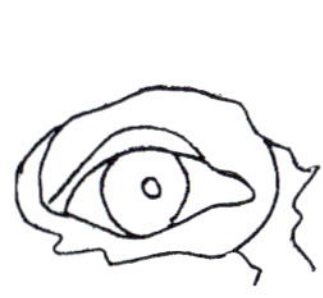 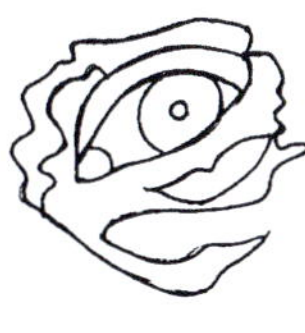 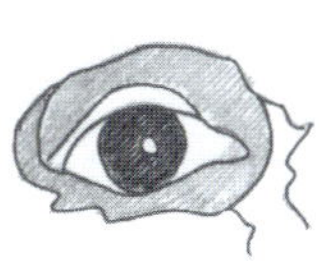 

3. Detailed eyes in which the white, the circular iris and dark pupil can be clearly seen. These eyes usually contain a small dot of bright reflected light in the iris. This adds the sparkle and is variable in shape.

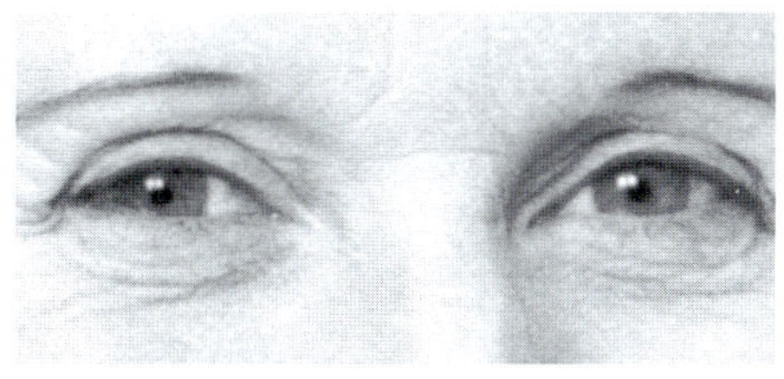   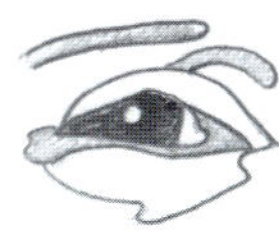 

With this type of eye you can often clearly see the skin folds of the upper eyelid, the rim of the lower lid, and possibly ' bags' of skin beneath the eye.

It is very important to trace these skin folds accurately as they give each eye its unique shape and character.

Eyes are not difficult to appliqué, although type 3 will take a little longer, as there will be more construction pieces.

In all eyes the coloured part, the iris, is uniformly circular .... but the amount you can see and its exact position depends on facial expression, age and the individual characteristics of each eye.

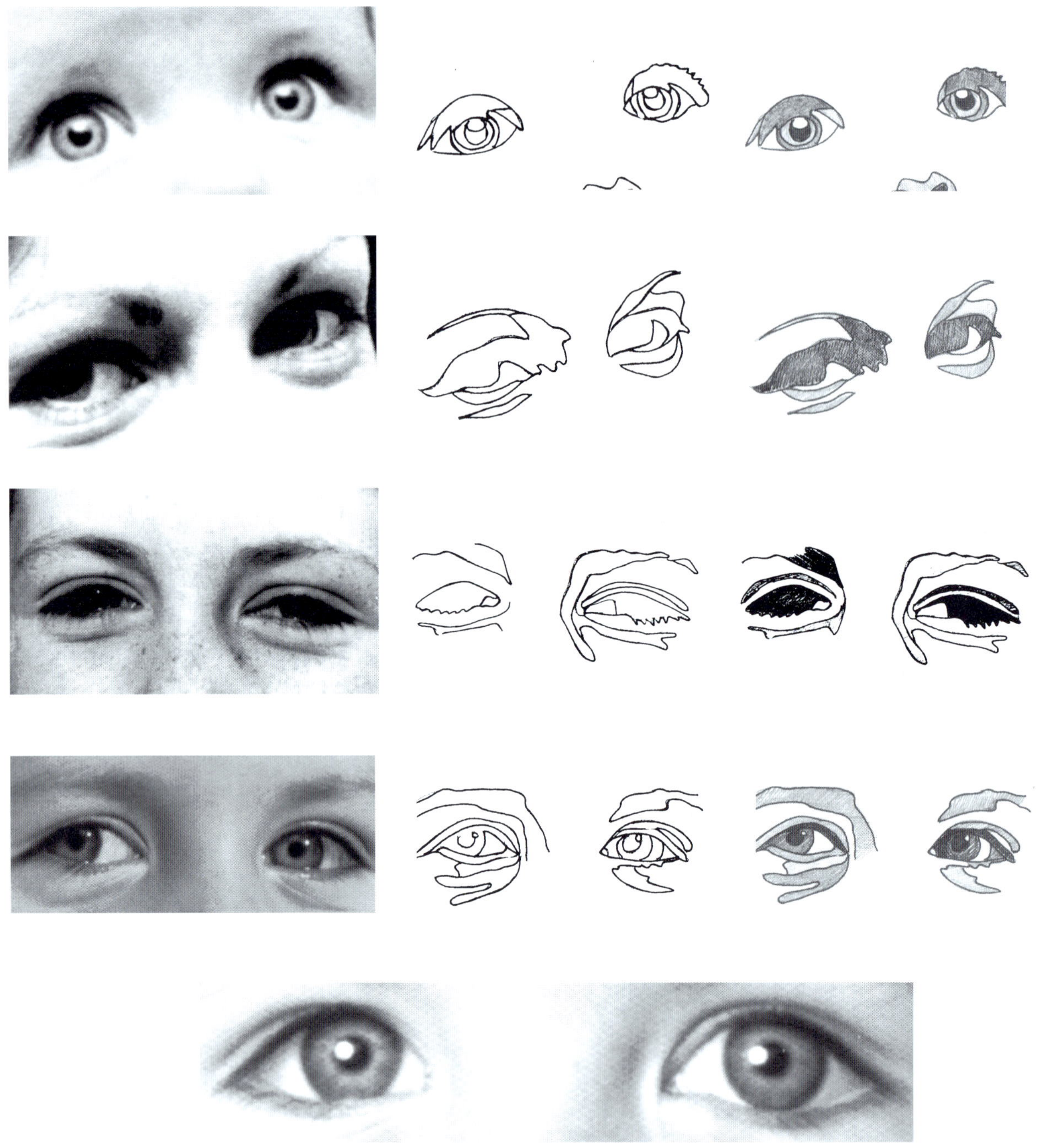

The black central spot, or pupil, is also uniformly circular ... but its size depends on the level of light shining into it at any given time.

Scientific studies show that we find eyes with larger pupils more attractive .... and our own pupils dilate when we are attracted ....
(so who will know if we help Nature a little by enlarging the pupils of our subject's eyes slightly?) But do not overdo it !!

'Ben Alec'
24 ins. x 30 ins.

by
Jenny Hipperson.

Harpenden,
Herts.

"Oupa"
Werner Jon Pfleughoeft.

20XII-21XII.
1885-1977.

20 x 20 ins.

By
Jane Plowman.

Bovingdon,
Herts.

" Ant"

24 x 26 1/2 ins.

By
the Author

"Honest Abe"

28 x 28 ins.

by Sue Martin.

Mouths and teeth.

The artist Whistler is reputed to have said ....
'a portrait is a painting in which there is something wrong with the mouth.'

There may be a great deal of truth in this observation as mouths, like eyes, can be difficult to get right when reproducing a face.

Trust what you see. ....

I wish that I had taken my own advice in 'Simplicity and Style, ' one of my early portrait attempts on page 83 ... where I tried to deviate from what I saw in the photo showing the formal pose and changed the mouth .... (to avoid including teeth as I assumed that they would be difficult .. wrong !).
This alteration changed Laura's expression .... making it rather hard.

The best rule is always ..
.. Only include what you can see .... do not deviate.
If you want a different expression ... take another photo.

Some features of mouths and lips can be predicted...

1. Children's lips have more bulge than adult's .... and 'Cupid's bow' is very pronounced in toddlers and babies.

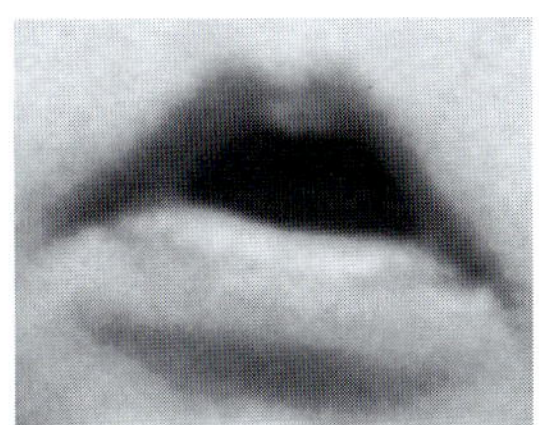

2. Male lips are usually thinner, flatter and more elongated than those of females ...

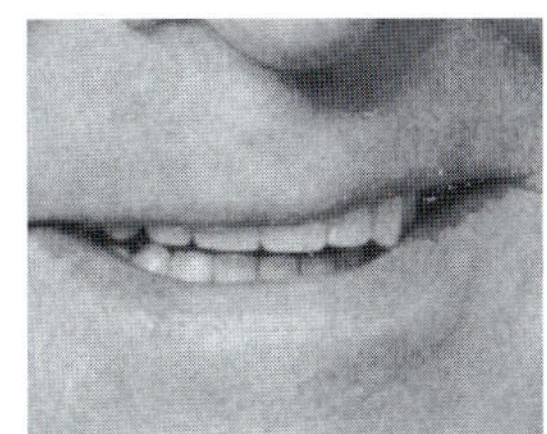

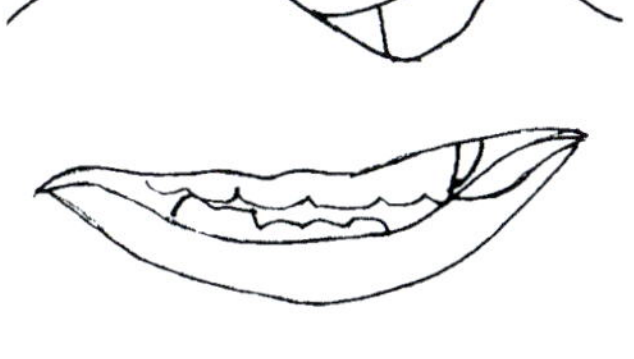

which generally have a more defined outline and colour ....
especially if wearing lipstick.

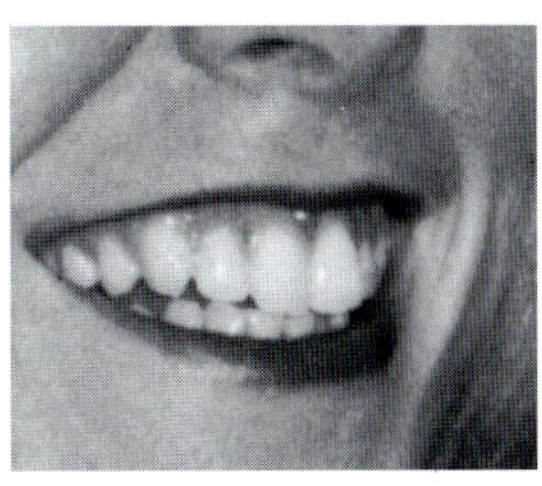

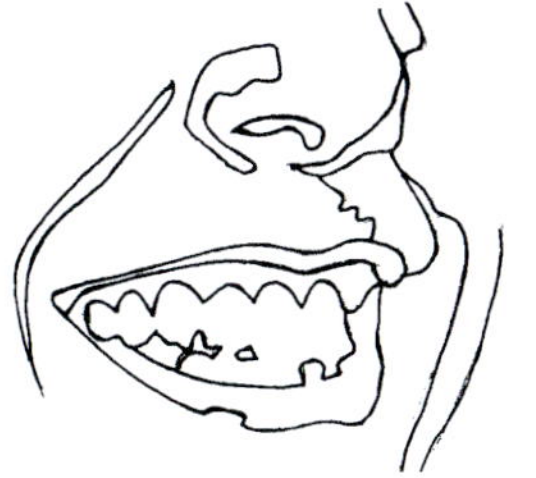

One lip may be more shadowed than the other ....usually the upper one.

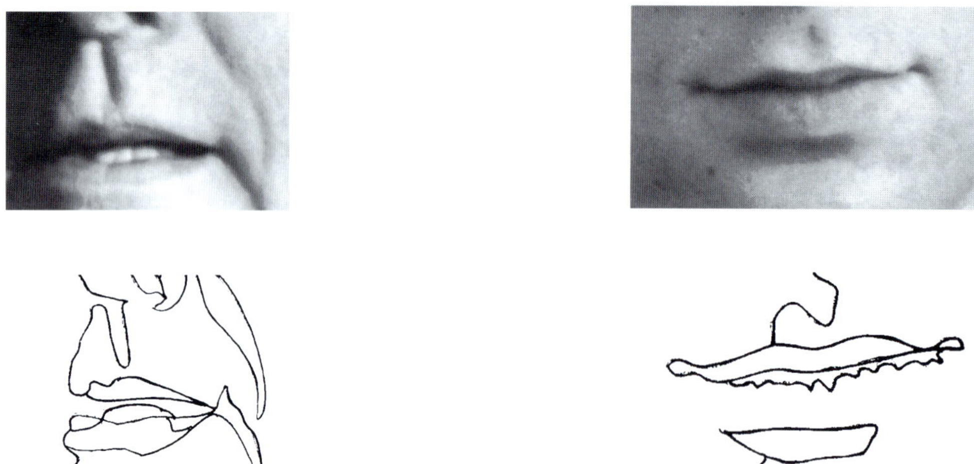

3. Teeth are not white. They are often darker than you might think, especially where they curve away to the corners of the mouth. The tooth area can be treated as one complete shape and left as such ....

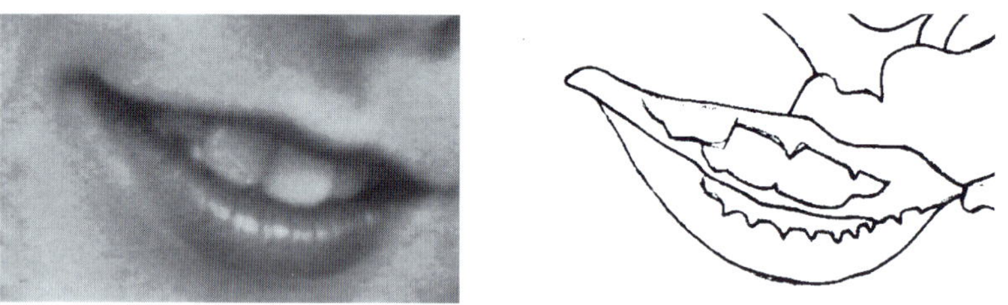

.... with no divisions between individual teeth ... or these can be lightly dotted in by pen. Heavily marking these divisions can be unflattering.

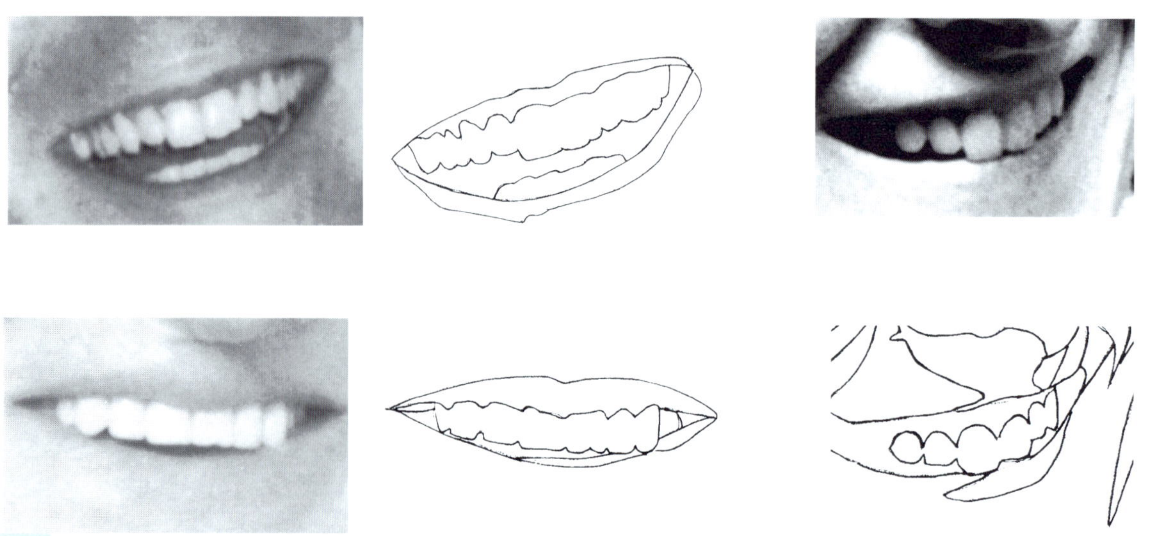

Noses.

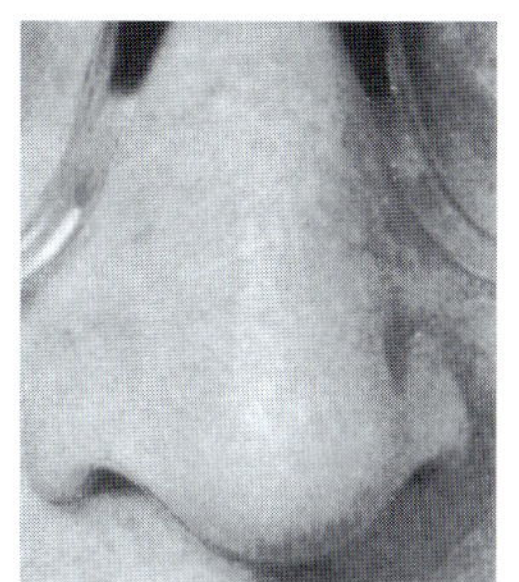

If noses are analysed too closely we cannot help but wonder at the design of these strange looking objects. They are often regarded as being difficult to draw ... but this is usually because a linear approach rather than a tonal one has been adopted.

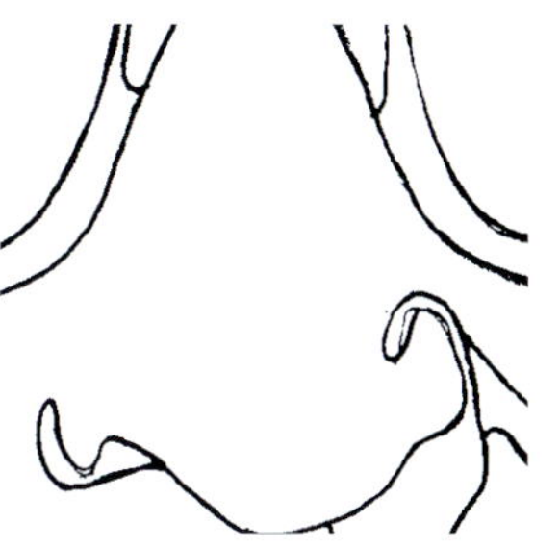

Do not fall into the trap of thinking in lines ..... turn that part of your brain off for a while .... and just trace around the important shadow shapes that you can see. It is often easier to make these observations and assess the differing tones more clearly if you squint through half closed eyes.

Generally, the bridge and the fleshy tip of the nose are the most strongly highlighted areas, while the outer 'wings' are slightly in shadow. The highlights are caused by the fact that the nose sticks out, catching the light ... and the skin is often smooth and slightly greasy. Emphasising this fact by tracing the shiny bits may not be particularly flattering.

There may be one shape which includes nose and cheek with no real line between them. Do not force the division if the photograph does not show one.

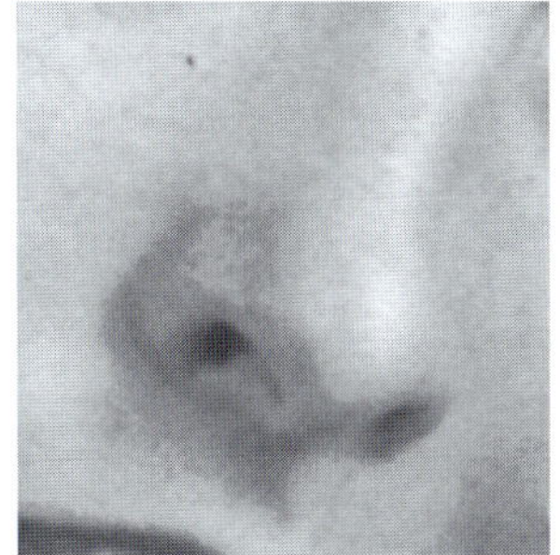

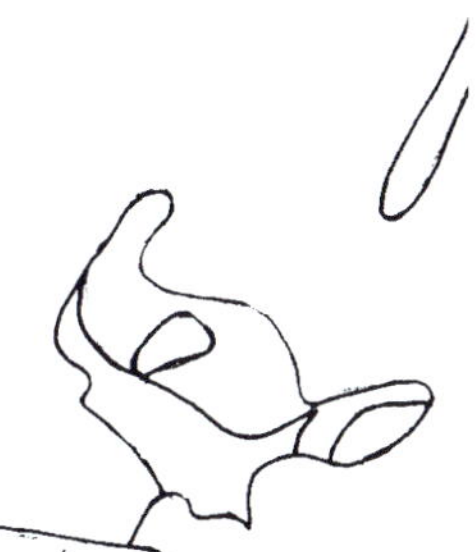

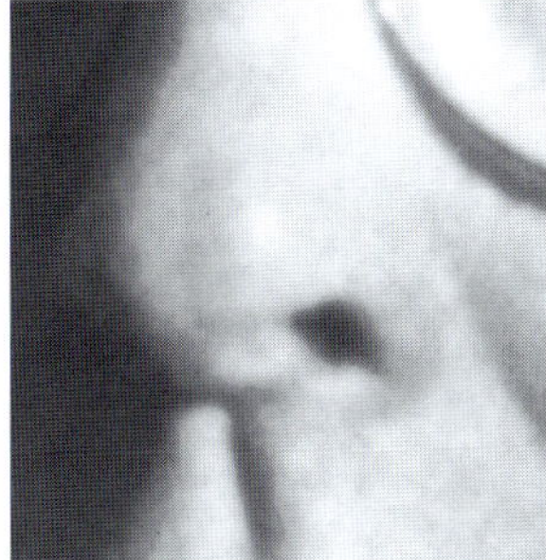

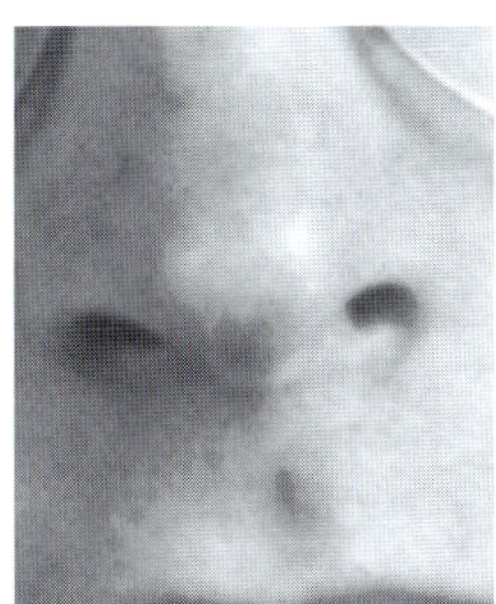

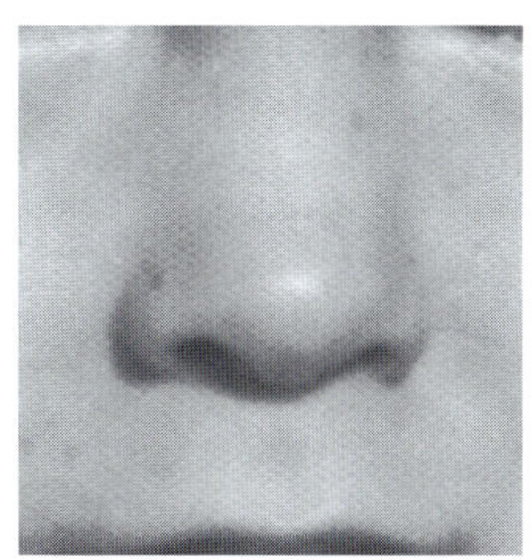

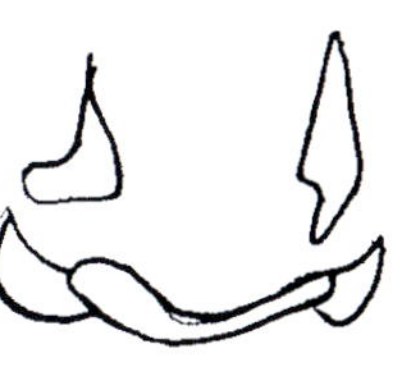

Hair.

Hair can have movement, texture, highlights and direction. It can sometimes look flat and all the same colour too. We can add the previous attributes if they cannot be found

Waves, shine and colour changes are the key factors when finding shapes.

A hairstyle will never be satisfactory as one big fabric shape.

Waves and curls .... if these exist our tracing can just follow their outlines and we can fill each curl with a different fabric. As the direction of the hair varies ... so too can the patterns on directional fabrics.

Shine ...... this will depend on tonal contrast between fabrics to achieve the desired effect .... the highlights being much lighter than the surrounding area. Shine tends to be more noticeable on straight hair ... with the light showing up at right angles to the direction of the hair. The pattern on fabric should always follow hair direction.

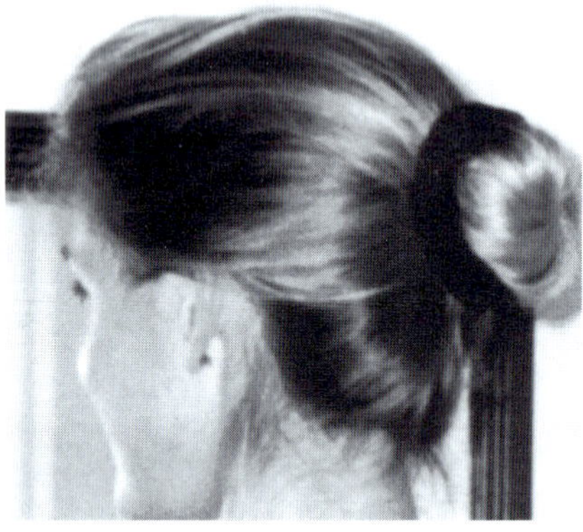

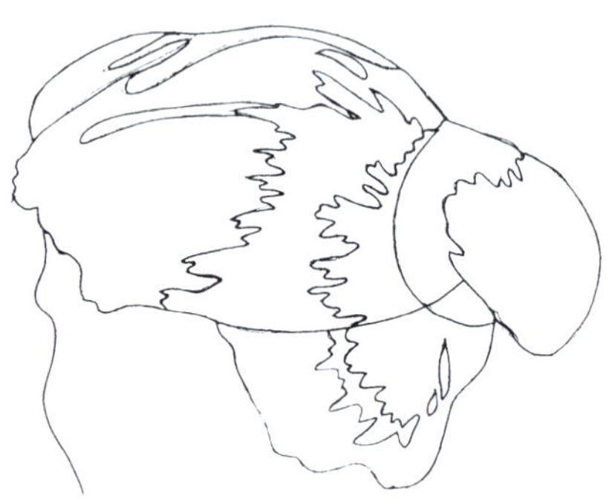

Colour changes ..... these can indicate colour differences, hair layers or, ... sometimes a thin covering allowing the scalp to show through .... often seen in shots of babies and older people. The first two can be traced as basic shapes, but the latter needs a little more thought. Avoid strong tonal contrasts between skin and hair fabrics ..... or if hair is really thin use a permanent pen to dot colour sparingly.

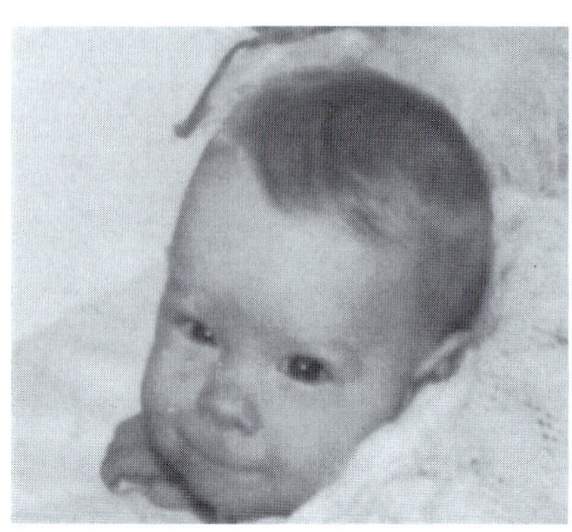

Tracing to create a working design.

After obtaining a suitable photocopy of the chosen photograph we need to use it to create an accurate line drawing of the image shapes. This we do by tracing. The easiest way to trace quickly and accurately is to use carbon paper for reproducing the greater part of the image, especially the parts that are an easy decision to include .... or contain fine detail.

1. Position the carbon paper .... carbon side down ... under the enlarged photocopy of the photo. .... on top of a blank sheet of paper.

2. Staple or pin the layers together at the top of the page. Paper clips may not prevent the pages from moving as you work, causing the production of multiple images. Anchoring the papers in this way will enable the copy and carbon to be lifted and accurately replaced as many times as required to check progress on the tracing as you work.

3. Using a mechanical lead pencil and applying firm pressure, draw around the main outline first. This will capture the subject and set up the correct positions for all other features.
Do not include every minute wiggle in the outline .... remember that the shapes you are tracing will have to be sewn. Where possible simplify and streamline.

4. Identify and draw around shapes that provide inside detail next ... the most important ones first ... followed by the less important. These shapes are the details that add interest to your subject, making it more realistic.

5. For the moment .... leave out all shapes that you are unsure about. Decisions to include or omit these can be made using the acetate a little later on.

The pencil line can be clearly seen on the photocopy making it easy to check where you have and have not drawn. This prevents the possibility of your skipping parts and leaving blanks.
(Pencil lines will be easy to erase should this be required.)

View your developing tracing as a jig-saw puzzle, or a painting by numbers canvas. It will be at its most boring, scrappy and unconvincing right now. **Do not get alarmed. Few of us would recognise familiar faces from photo negatives.** Just keep on believing that if you have traced the lines accurately all will be well as soon as you 'pour the colour back into the empty shapes' later on by filling each with fabric.

6 To complete the tracing ..... place an acetate sheet on top of the photocopy and, using an overhead projector pen, draw around any shapes that you were unsure about.

7. Always include one or two shapes that you have already traced as reference points whilst using acetate ...... these will enable you to match the carbon and acetate tracings accurately to judge the effect.

8. In order to help you decide if each shape should be included, or not, remove the photocopy and carbon, and place the acetate on top of the tracing.
The pen lines on the acetate can be viewed in combination with the carbon lines to judge the overall finished effect.

9. It can help to have several acetate sheets ..... so that you can try out different shape combinations on each. Lay them in turn on the carbon drawing to find the one that you like best.

10. Remove any mistakes that occur when drawing on the acetate with a tissue folded into a point around a damp 'cotton wool bud .
The tissue will collect all the black ink and can be refolded at intervals to create a new clean point as required.
Very fine details can be erased using this method with no disruption of nearby lines.

11. Always keep the original photo and photocopy beside you as you work, consulting them if in doubt about anything at all. Checking details in two different sizes can help with the decisions to include something or to leave it out. Squinting through half closed eyes can be helpful.

12. Intense observation is tiring, especially if you are not used to it. When we get tired, we can unconsciously revert to drawing from memory and stop tracing what we see.
Take frequent breaks ..... everything will be exactly as you left it when you return ... but your brain will be rested ... and your eyes will be sharper.

13. Pin the photocopy and your tracing side by side on a wall or board and study them from a distance ...... e.g. across a room ... this can provide a different perspective. Distance can help you to compare the degree of similarity.

14. When you are finished ... if you have some details that you choose to use on the acetate, clear tape it on to the carbon tracing in the correctly matched position. The combined image is now ready to enlarge to the actual size of the intended appliqué.

Enlarging to working size.

For most projects the traced size is too small to use for our actual size work. Appliqué is always easier to complete with larger pieces. The smaller the shapes used ... the harder they will become to manipulate and the greater the skill level required to piece them successfully

Different sizes suit different needleworkers. If you are inexperienced, think big and use an image with a limited number of shapes for a first project. Generally the bigger the fabric pieces, the easier they will be to manage.

Most images, however, will contain some very small pieces. As long as there are not too many of them they will not be a problem.

To enlarge the design to actual size return to the photocopy shop where you need to take ***a black and white*** copy of the combined acetate and carbon tracing.

The maximum size that can be achieved on a standard machine in England is approx. 16 3/4 x 23 1/2 ins = 43 x60 cm. This final enlargement will be the master copy from which a freezer paper pattern will be traced and then cut up to create the templates.

A machine used for duplicating architect's plans can create much bigger copies approx. 33x 47ins. = 84 x 120 cm. Many photocopy shops have such machines. They can instantly enlarge from the black and white photocopy of your design.

If this is not possible there are two alternative methods ....

1. Drawing a grid over your design and a corresponding larger grid of the required size on the dull side of freezer paper ... then accurately copying the contents of each small square on the design into the corresponding large square on the freezer paper. This is efficient but labour intensive and slow.

2. Enlarging can also be achieved by cutting the design into separate sections and individually photocopy enlarging each one before clear taping them together again. Photocopying always causes a slight distortion of the image, so lines crossing joins may need to be redrawn.

Turning the design into templates.

Once the line drawing is finished and photocopied to size, the next stage is to trace it once again, this time onto the dull side of freezer paper. The photocopied tracing will be your master plan. It is the 'map' which will help if you lose your way whilst appliquéing. The freezer paper tracing will be cut up to create exact templates for each fabric section. Seam allowances are not of concern at this stage, they will be included later when cutting the fabric.

Anchor the freezer paper on top of the working design with pins, or staples, to prevent movement. Trace every line clearly. It is vitally important to maintain accuracy at every stage in the technique .... so do not rush. The lines you trace now will control the shape of every piece of fabric in the appliqué. Even minor differences can cause noticeable variations from the original, decreasing the possibility of achieving a good likeness. Completing this tracing on top of a light box may aid accuracy.

Registration Marks.

When the tracing is finished add registration marks. These take the form of tiny lines which cross every line in the drawing at frequent intervals. Marking lines in this way is invaluable when re-assembling sections once they have been cut apart. Make sure that you do not miss any lines out.

Adding such marks may seem like a chore ..... but it only takes minutes and will enable the fabric shapes to be matched with ease once assembly begins.

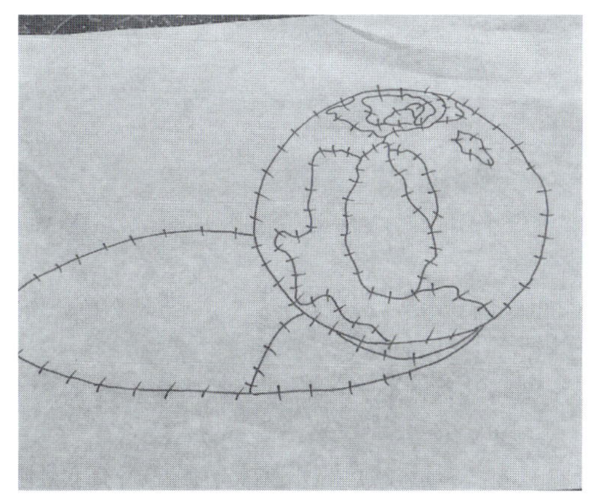

Label all shapes as light, medium or dark. This is also a good time to double check that all shapes in the drawing are 'islands'. Shading shapes with pencil can help highlight any which may have incomplete outlines.

Freezer paper stabilises the fabric to which it is stuck, preventing it changing shape, or stretching. You can choose to follow, or ignore, the fabric grain.
If you wish to follow the grain ..... draw a series in vertical pencil lines at intervals across the drawing at this stage. When the shapes are cut apart you can use these lines as grain indicators.

Choosing suitable fabrics.

100% cotton is the fabric of choice for this technique. As all projects are different, it is impossible to give accurate fabric requirements. When shopping for fabric it is better to have small quantities of lots of different colours to create choice .... than a large quantity of a few colours.
Plains, hand dyed and small patterns work best.

Few artists would paint a picture without a range of paints to choose from. You will need a palette of colour too. Many shapes in a project will be very small so check out your scrap bag before you rush for the shops ... or swap scraps with friends.

Always look at both the front and back of fabrics ..... many are useable on both sides and you can extend your palette with two options for the price of one.
The wrong side is usually 1 or 2 tones lighter than the right side.

Deciding on your colour palette ....
possible choices are ....

1. True life colours ...

Fabric colours can be chosen regardless of whether the original photo is in full colour or not. If it is black and white or sepia you can invent the natural colours.
Colouring the line drawing can help with your choices.

2. Sepia ...

Looking at old photos will demonstrate that sepia colours can vary from light cream to dark chocolate, in the same way as a the greyscale already shown. (Don't forget that a colour photocopy machine can convert modern colour photos to sepia, imitating an old fashioned look ready for you to copy).

3. Monochromatic ...

You can choose to create your picture in a scale of any one colour ....
e.g. tones of green or blue.

4. Wild colours ...

The sky is the limit here. Think of the sorts of wild colours used in advertising. and heat imaging. You have already identified all the image shapes, now they are just waiting to have a colour, or a coloured pattern 'poured ' into each one.

Having an understanding of tone makes the selection of fabric colours easier for projects.

It is unnecessary to look for up to ten tonal values in any one picture.
We can certainly reproduce a very satisfactory likeness with far less .... certainly four or five would be quite sufficient.
Mentally divide your picture into 6 different significant coloured areas ... e.g.

1. Skin colours.
2. Hair colours.
3. Clothes.
4. Background.
5. Optional border or frame.
6. Eyes .... teeth .... lips ..... accessories.

Identify the darkest and lightest parts of each coloured area and estimate how far apart they are on the tonal scale. The closer they are .... the fewer different fabric colours are needed. However, always consider using several fabrics which have different patterns within one tone, as this will increase interest, variety and texture.

The highest number of skin tones I have ever used in a face is five ......
so I needed to find a fabric that was my darkest dark .... another that was my lightest light ... and three in between.
Remembering that the wrong side of many fabrics is quite useable and often about two tones lighter than the right side ... that many fabrics change colour value across the width, and also that you do not need large quantities of any one fabric, the requirements for these projects need not be demanding.

Apply the same logic to the other significant colour areas.

When you have established the number of fabrics in each colour area ....
label the freezer paper shapes to correspond, before they are cut apart.

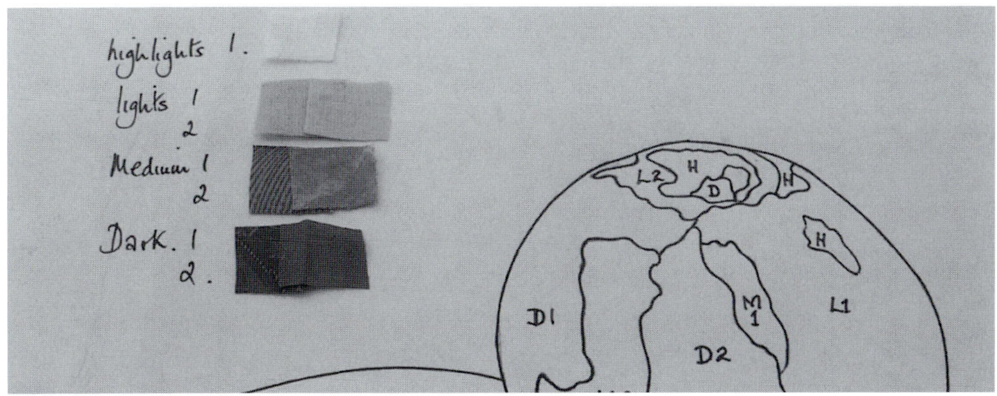

Styling Hair.

To be successful in creating appliqué hair it is vital to make the fabric work extra hard at providing almost all the detail. In just the same way as there are suitable 'skin' fabrics there are also suitable 'hair' fabrics.

If a range of 'hair patterned' fabric does not immediately spring to mind, do not worry. There are lots of great fabrics to be found ... if we go shopping thinking 'hair' .... and are prepared to do a little lateral thinking.

Abstract patterns ... grass patterns, wood grain patterns etc. can be ideal and often, if we are lucky they will be available in several colour choices.
The colour in some fabrics can change in density across the width providing a range of variations within a short length.

If the right pattern is found but the colour is wrong ... change it by dyeing with commercial dye ... or tea or coffee ... or car spray paint. Textured patterns can be printed on fabric by stencilling, potato cuts, sponging, or computer printed patterns.

Natural hair is never one solid colour. It contains many subtle tints and shades. Blue and brown may be present in black hair .... honey and red in brown hair .... brown, gold and grey in blond hair .... and blue, white, grey and beige in grey hair. Modern hair dyes can create more unexpected colours !!
(see 'Ant' on page 35.)

Collect lots of fabric in small amounts, creating a 'possibly useful' palette of colours ..... experiment with both patterns and plains, mixing them to generate interest, styling and highlights.

Beards, eyebrows and moustaches need 'hair' patterned fabrics too, unless they are sparse and stubbly. In this case a light dotting with pen can create a more realistic effect where fabric could seem too solid.
(See 'Ant's' beard page 35.)

The silhouette of a hairstyle is always going to be hard edged ......
any stray wisps will have to be added in embroidery, or by pen. Tightly curled hair can be indicated by a tightly curled quilting pattern ... or even couched wool or braid for a 3D effect.

Tip !

Line patterns which are suitable for reproducing hair can be computer scanned from a flat source .... e.g. a drawing ... section of pattern from fabric ..... a photo of tree bark, grass etc. (bluebell leaves illustrated) and then computer printed onto plain fabric in a suitable colour. Iron freezer paper to the wrong side of the plain fabric to stabilise it before running it through the printer. Remember ... that the patterned fabric produced will not be washable as computer printer inks are not permanent.

Fabric patterns and colours which would be suitable for recreating hair.

Take some facial make-up with you when choosing skin coloured fabric ....
(in this case compressed powder).
As you can see good colours for fair skin will never be found amongst the pinks.

Darker coloured skin may show a larger variation in tone due to different amounts of pigmentation and the effects of bright light.

Thinking about fabric colours as if they were a greyscale highlights the lack of mid-tones in this selection.

Freezer paper templates.

Every shape in the freezer paper image will be cut apart from its neighbour to make templates

but not all at once !!!

The appliqué will be built up bit by bit. Do not cut all the design apart at this stage, as it is much easier to work with a small area at a time. This also ensures that small pieces do not get lost.
The following points are worth bearing in mind as you cut ...

Where you begin doesn't matter.....
..... *accuracy does.*

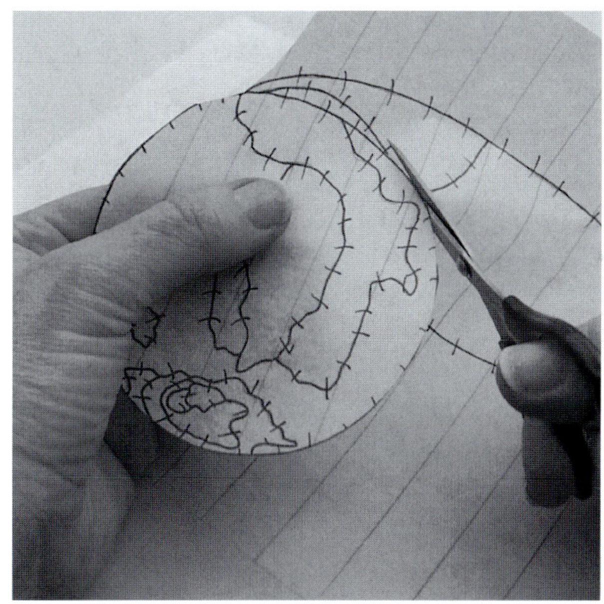

1. Begin by removing a manageable section from the image ......
(maybe containing four, or five shapes) where there seems to be a natural break in the design ...
e.g. a hairline, where skin meets clothes, or a complete item.

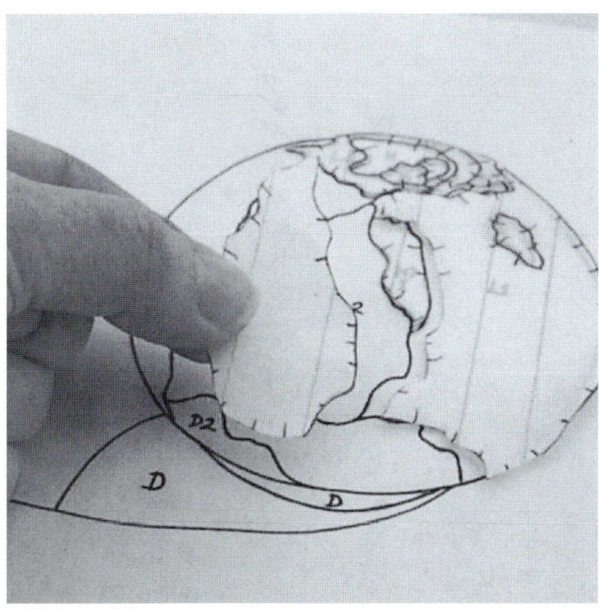

2. Use small, pointed, very sharp scissors and cut smoothly along the drawn lines. Cut slowly ..... laying the individual shapes in their correct position on top of the master pattern.

(Lay an acetate sheet on top of the cut pieces of paper to stop them from being blown away in a draught.) ...... or keep an envelope at hand to collect them in.

3. Cut wavy lines by swivelling the paper around the scissor blades. Practice cutting very small 'U ' shapes.

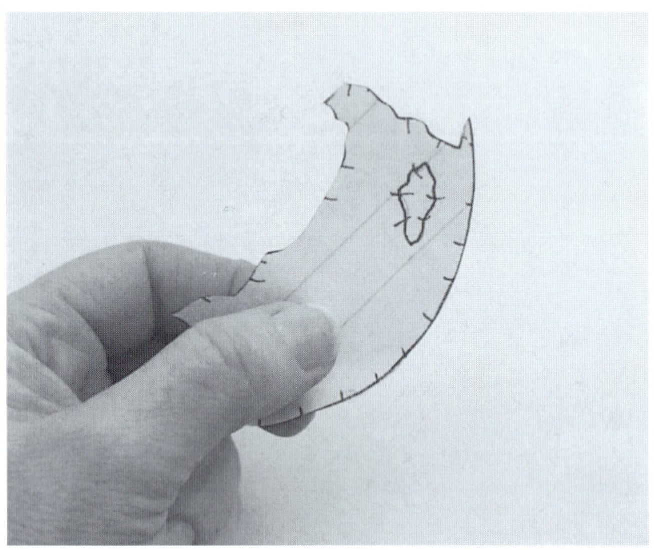

5. Do not cut out small 'islands' contained within a larger island at this stage.
See page 59.

If nearing a place where a line changes direction, do not cut too far back on the scissor blade,

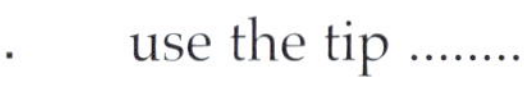

.... use the tip ....

...... Should the scissors accidentally close, cutting along the whole length of the blade, it cannot make too long a cut.

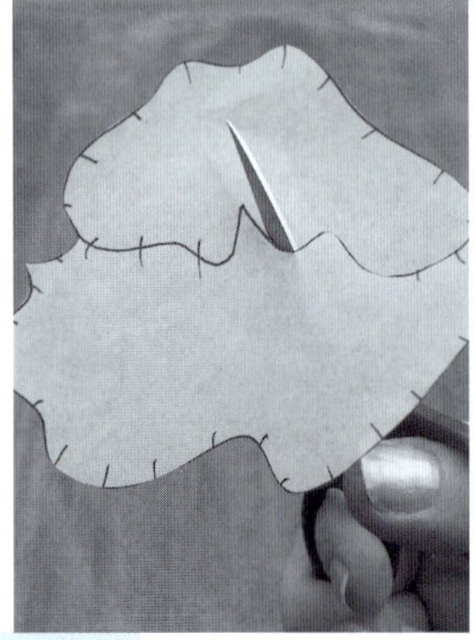

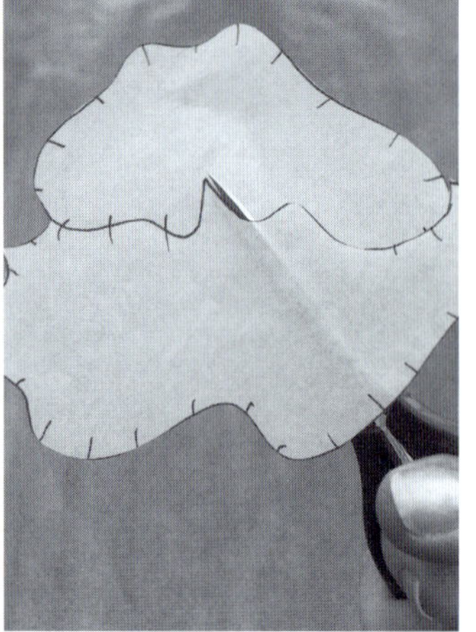

If an accidental cut is made ...... mend with clear tape on the dull side of the paper and re-cut.

Cutting fabric shapes.

Having chosen your fabrics ... washed them if necessary and spray starched them .... you are ready to get going.

Iron each freezer paper shape ....

shiny side down onto the ***right side*** of the fabric.

Ironing Freezer paper to fabric....

Test iron your freezer paper to your fabric before you embark on a project. The temperature of the iron will make a great difference to the ease with which the paper adheres .... too cool ..... and it falls off prematurely, ... too hot ..... and it can become difficult to remove.

Since all irons vary, exact guidelines cannot be given. Start testing around 'warm' rather than 'hot'.

Freezer paper can also behave differently when used with fabric of differing fibre content and finishes.

As a general rule 100% cotton fabric is the easiest to use and gives the best results.

1. If you have decided not to follow the fabric grain ......
the direction in which the paper shapes are placed on the fabric will not matter
.......they can be placed to make the most economical use of the fabric.

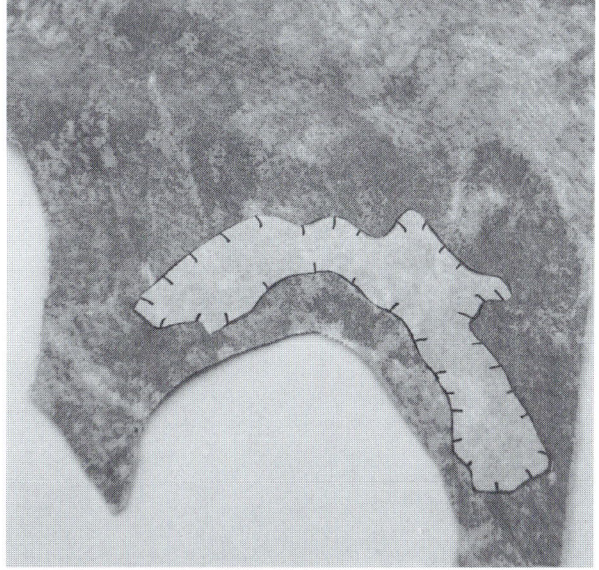

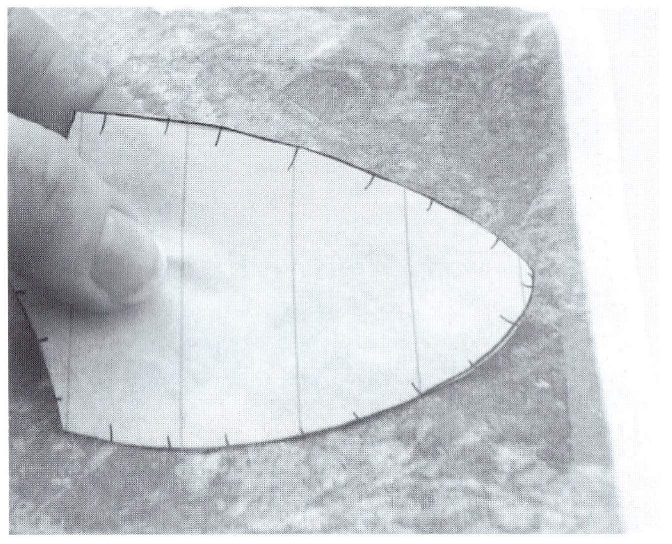

2. Otherwise match the parallel pencil lines (page 45) to the thread direction.

3. If several paper shapes are to be ironed to the same colour fabric, position them ***a generous 1/4 in. apart*** ..... to enable fabric allowances to be cut between them.

4. Cut the fabric allowing a generous 1/8 in./ ·5 mm. margin around each paper shape. Always allow this margin ... unless otherwise instructed ... even though you will be cutting part, or all of it away later.

Using fusible web.

The next stage of the technique requires the use of fusible web .. i.e. Bondaweb™.

To secure the fusible web to the paper backing.

As already pointed out, fusible web which has become separated from its backing paper is difficult to use. Here is an easy method of preventing this from happening ....

1. With paper side uppermost, lay a piece of Bondaweb ™ on top of the non-stick sheet on an ironing board.

2. Check that the heat setting on the iron is no higher than 'warm'.
It is a good idea to experiment with a small piece of fusible to gauge the best setting on your particular iron.

3. Lightly iron the Bondaweb™ through the backing paper to the sheet to warm it.
It will temporarily adhere to the non-stick sheet.

4. Roll the Bondaweb™ together with the ironing sheet and place the roll in a freezer for a few minutes. The intense cold will harden the fusible and speed up the separation from the non-stick sheet. Leaving it to cool at room temperature may take considerably longer.

5. If the iron temperature was correct the fusible will easily fall away from the ironing sheet. If it was too hot and parts are still stuck .... do not pull ... this will tear the fusible. Use firm pressure from a blunt instrument e.g. the handle of a rotary cutter, to rub over these parts through the paper against the board. This action should break the bond without causing damage to the web.

The fusible side will look shiny by comparison with an untreated sample.
(This also makes it easier to distinguish between paper and fusible when it is cut).

The fusible web will now be well adhered to the paper, ready to be cut into strips.

The paper will still peel away when required, after fusing to fabric.

(It is worth using this method to try to rehabilitate previously purchased Bondaweb™ which has separated, ... after all you have nothing to lose ....
as once the layers have fallen apart it is very fragile and difficult to handle.)

Cutting Fusible strips.

1. Lay the Bondaweb™ paper side down on a cutting board and cut strips of approx 1/8 in. ... 5 mm. wide ...... using a rotary cutter.
Cut these by eye. They do not need straight edges or to be accurate.
Approx. is fine.

2. Select two neighbouring design shapes. Taking the darker colour, cut off the fabric allowance along the length of the edge which is common to both shapes.
(See page 58 for 'darker colour rule'
If they are a similar tone it does not matter which shape you trim.)

<u>Do not trim both !</u>

3. Place the trimmed shape, wrong side up, on top of the non-stick ironing sheet. Iron a Bondaweb ™ strip, or strips, along the trimmed edge, placing it so that the strip slightly overlaps the fabric edge.
Bonding the edge will prevent fraying.

4. Working from the right side trim away surplus Bondaweb™ exactly to the paper's edge.

Peel and discard the paper backing from the Bondaweb™.

(It is much easier to cut away the surplus *before* peeling the paper away.)

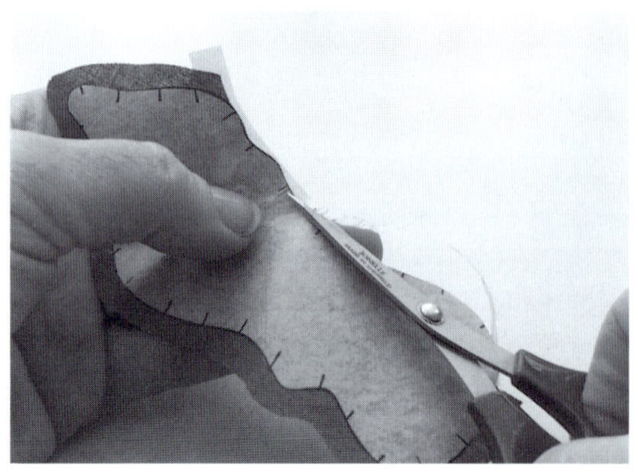

Joining fabric shapes.

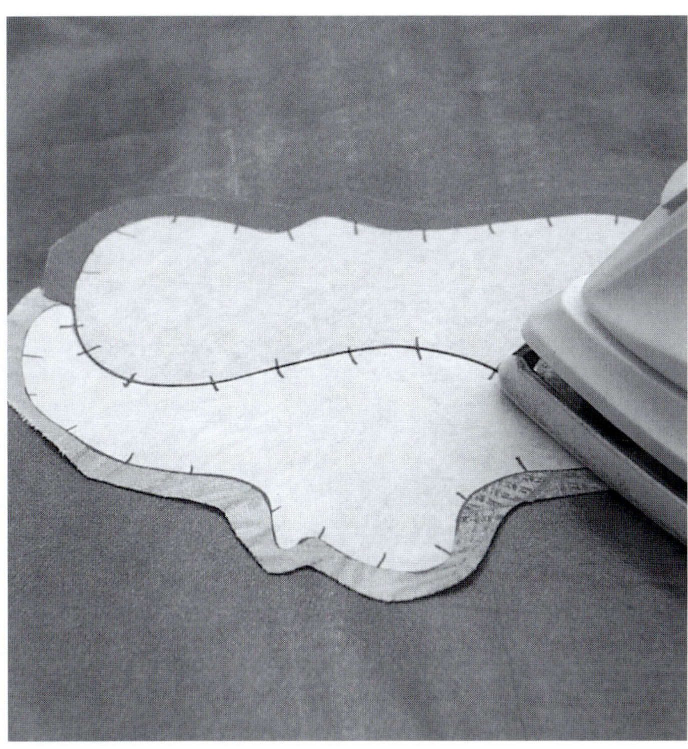

5. With right sides of fabric uppermost ..... place the trimmed shape on top of the fabric allowance of the other .... accurately matching the edges of both papers.

They should fit together with the registration lines perfectly lined up.
When the shapes are correctly positioned ... iron the join, through the freezer paper, fusing both shapes with a firm bond.

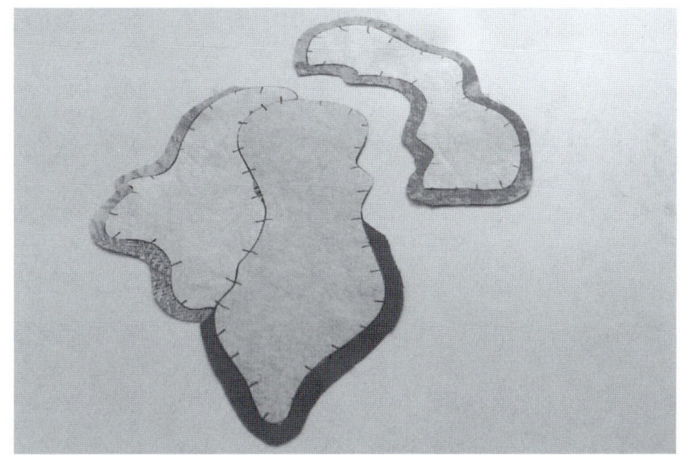

6. Choose another neighbouring shape and repeat ....

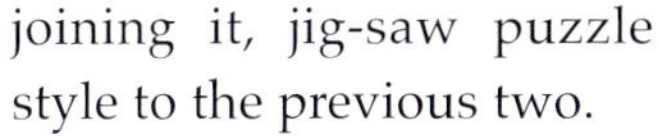

joining it, jig-saw puzzle style to the previous two.

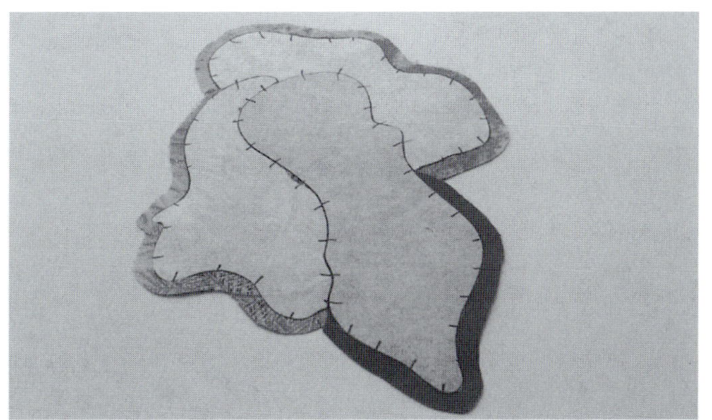

Continue to add shapes building up the image, cutting more freezer paper templates as required.

Ensure that you do not trim the fabric allowance from anywhere other than ***the common edge*** of any shape. If you do, you may accidentally remove an allowance vital to the completion of later join

Tip !

Should this accidentally happen .... separate the freezer paper and fabric from the offending section ...... and cut a replacement fabric shape using the same paper template ....
Freezer paper will peel off and re-stick several times before losing its 'stickability.'

Tip !

If you accidentally destroy or lose a paper shape, ... simply trace a replacement from the master photocopy on scrap freezer paper and continue.

Tip !

If you are unsure regarding a colour choice .... bond the fabric shape lightly in place ... temporarily remove the freezer paper to check the effect ....
if you do not like it, gently break the bond and remove the fabric.
Peel the freezer paper from the rejected fabric ... and iron it to an alternative colour.

'dark fabric is always placed on top of light'

This is an important rule ....

The edge of each fabric shape is not turned under .... it is a raw fabric edge which will be enclosed by stitching ... so it is only one layer of fabric in thickness. If the edge of a light fabric is placed on top of a dark, there is a strong possibility that the dark fabric allowance will show through on the right side of the work, especially when the white batting/wadding is placed behind it. This can spoil an image possibly giving the appearance of '5 o'clock shadow.'

Remember ....

The fusible only holds the fabric pieces together to enable the stitching to be completed. It serves the same purpose as pins in conventional patchwork.

The image must be completely fused together before stitching can begin.

Alternative methods for joining shapes.

There are two other methods of joining shapes in addition to the previous edge to edge system. Both are used when one shape is surrounded by another either totally or partially. The choice between these methods will depend upon the sizes of the shapes involved. In this method the 'dark on light' rule still applies.

Method 1

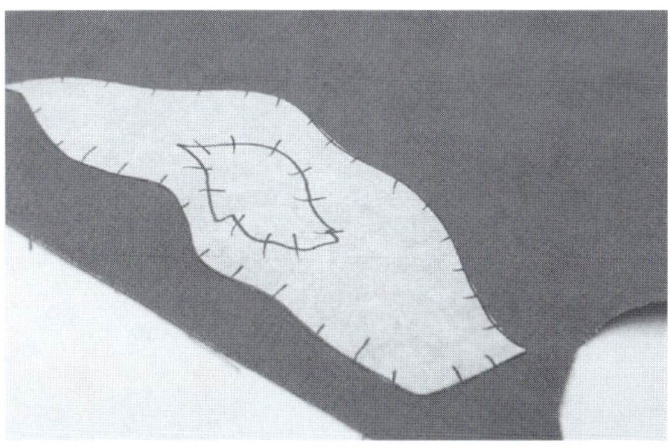

a. Do not cut the shapes apart. Iron the paper template containing both shapes to the outer shape fabric. Cut out with allowance.

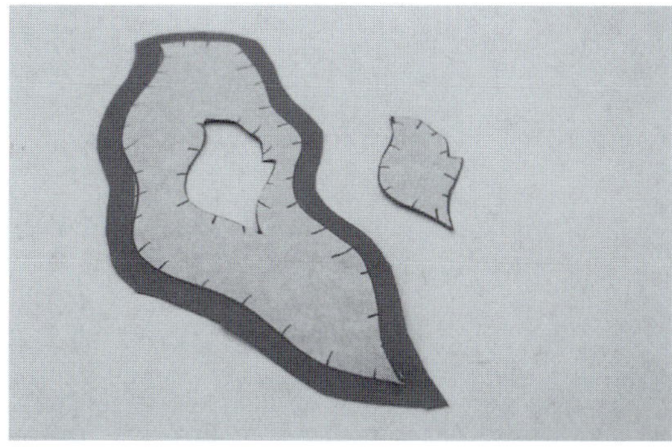

b. Carefully cut through both paper and fabric to remove the inner shape.

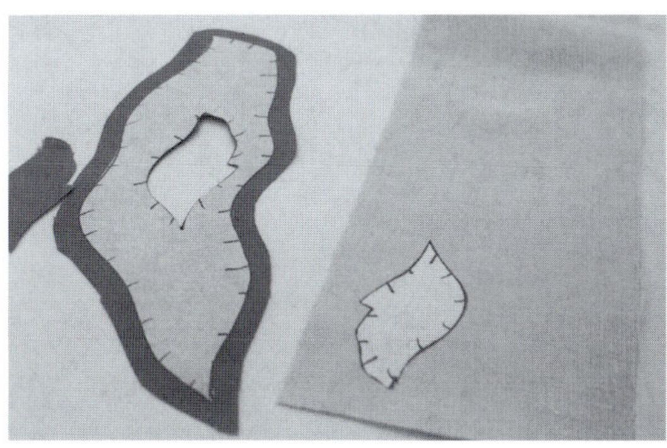

c. Separate the inner shape paper template and iron it to a new lighter coloured fabric.

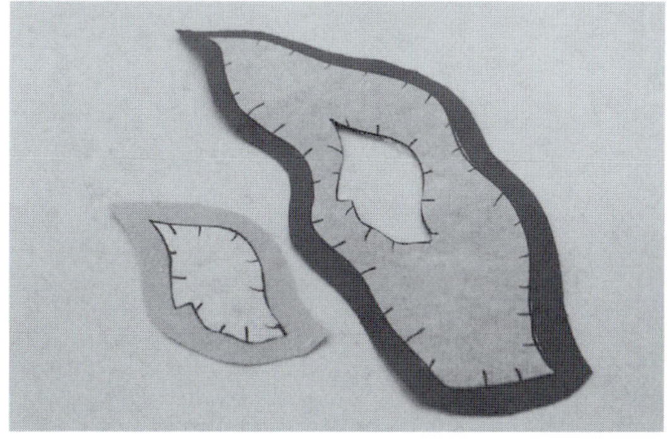

d. Cut inner shape with fabric allowance.

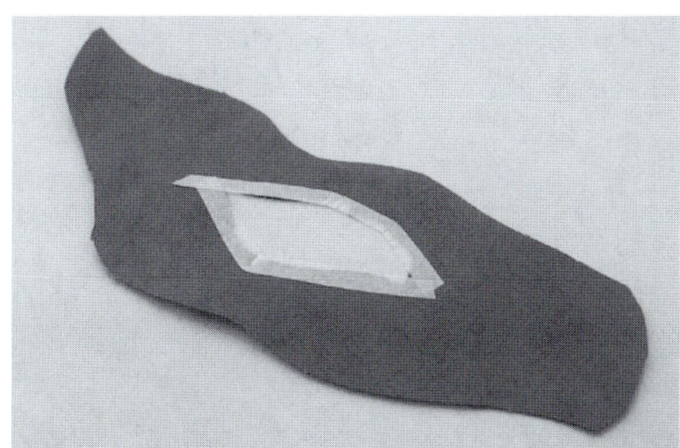

e. Bondaweb ™ around the rim of the hole in the outer shape on the wrong side.
Trim surplus fusible and remove the paper backing.

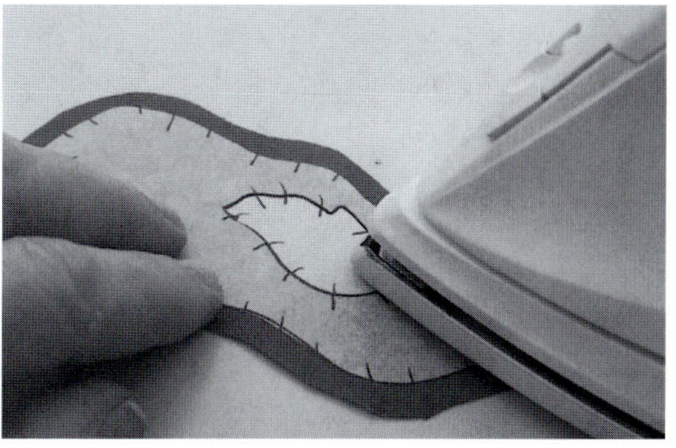

f. Place the outer shape on top of inner ...
matching registration marks ....
iron to bond ready for stitching.

Method 2 for smaller shapes.

In this method the dark on light rule need not apply.

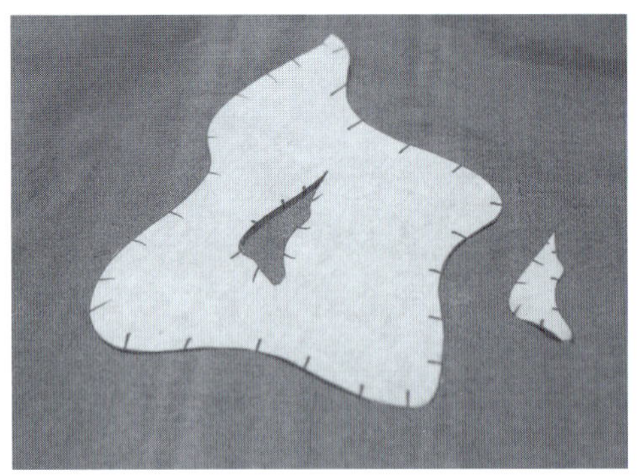

a. Cut out the inner shape from the freezer paper .

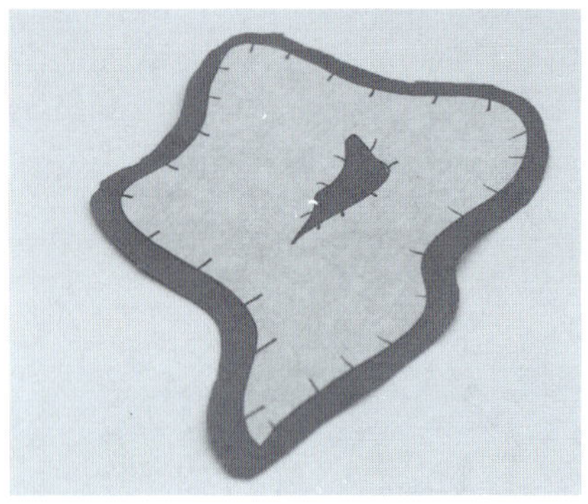

b. Iron the paper template for the the outer shape to the fabric.

d. Cut a piece of Bondaweb slightly larger than the inner shape ...
iron it to the wrong side of the chosen fabric.
See page 61 ..... Tip!

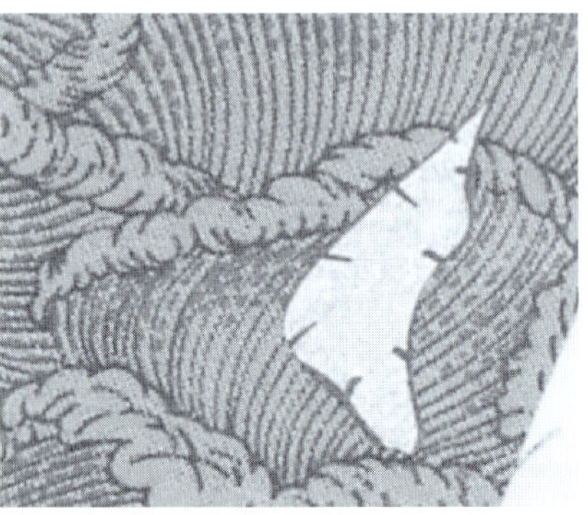

e. Iron the inner shape template to the right side of the fabric ... alighning it over the Bondaweb ™ on the back.

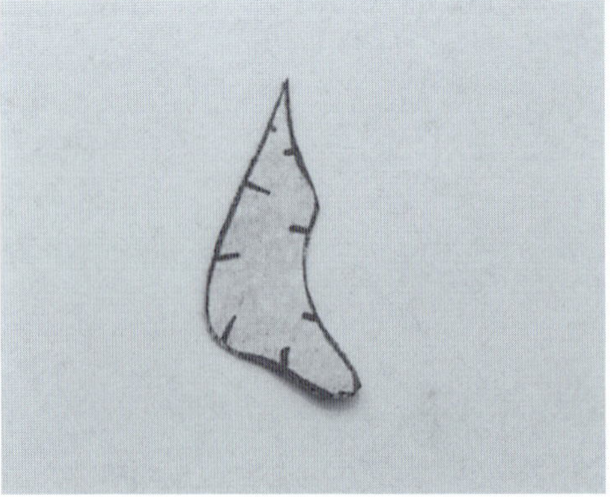

f. Cut out the inner shape exactly to the paper ... no fabric allowance..

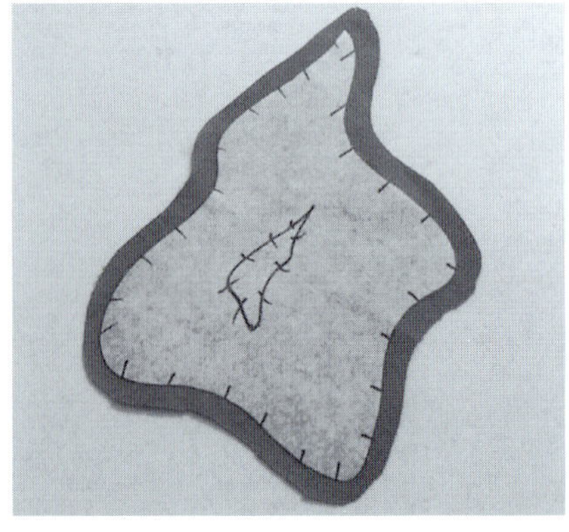

g. Position, match and bond inner shape on the right side of outer shape ready for stitching.

Assembling detailed eyes.

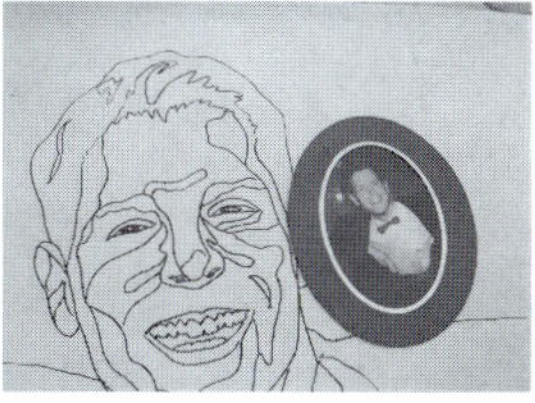

Detailed eyes ...... (type 3 on page 31) can appear daunting to assemble. However, they are not difficult if the following steps are followed ......

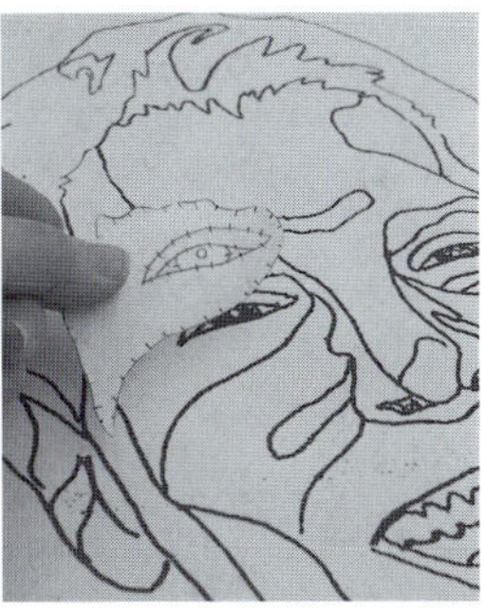

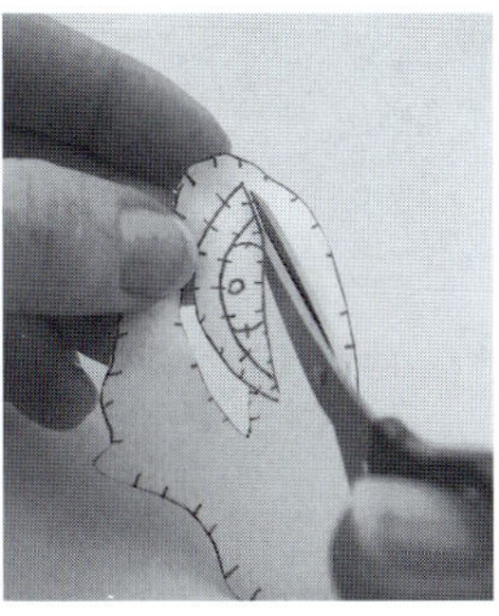

1. From the freezer paper tracing cut out the skin area which surrounds the eye.
Cut the eye and the eyelid from this section.

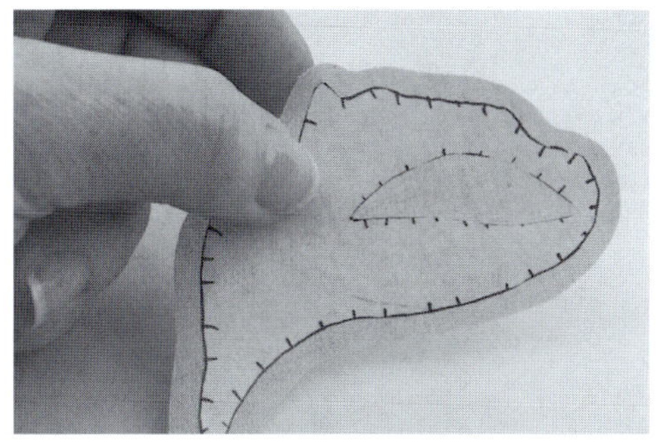

2. Iron template of skin area to skin fabric. Cut out with fabric allowance but do not cut out the eye 'hole' from the fabric.

3. Apply fusible web to back of eyelid fabric ... as described below...
cut eyelid shape from freezer paper eye.

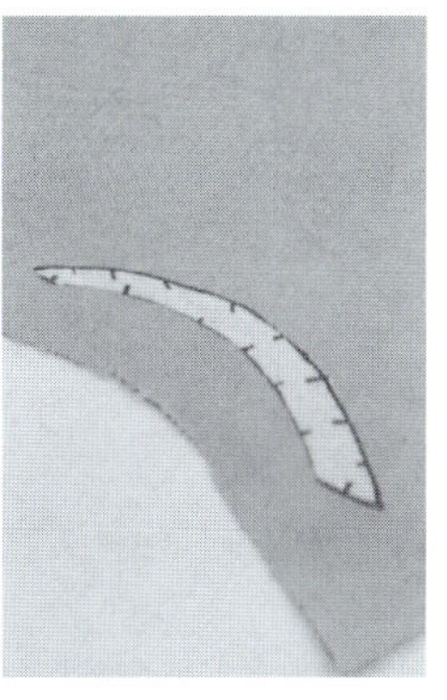

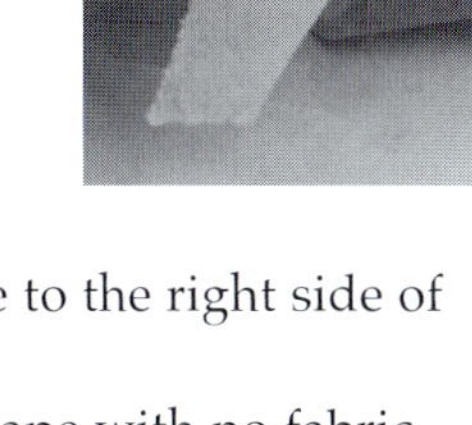

4. Iron eyelid template to the right side of fabric...
and cut out eyelid shape with no fabric allowance ... as described below.

Tip !

When dealing with very small shapes ... .
it is easier to iron fusible to the wrong side of a piece of fabric which is larger than you will need ....
leaving the backing paper in place .... **before** ......
ironing the freezer paper template to the right side.
This makes the fabric easier to hold and manipulate, enabling the small shape to be cut more accurately. No further trimming of the fusible will then be required.

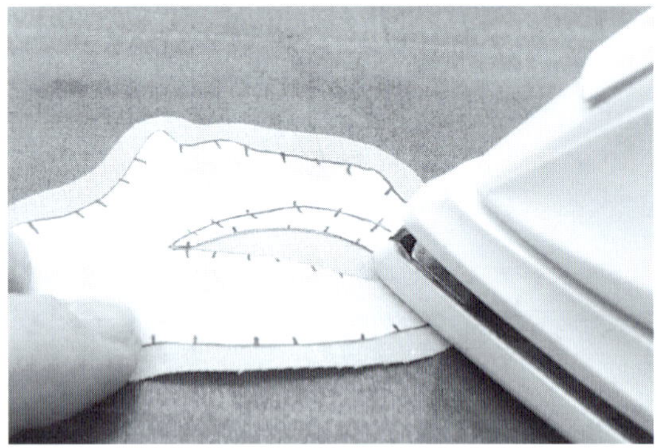

5. Remove fusible backing paper.
Position eyelid, matching registration marks ..... and bond in place in eye hole.

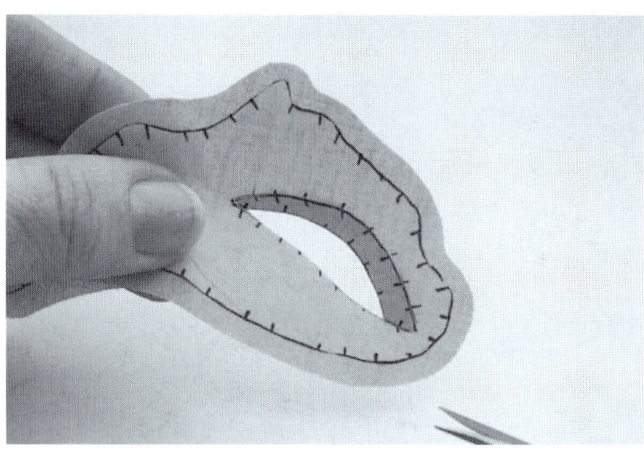

6. Cut out the skin fabric from the remaining area of the eye hole.

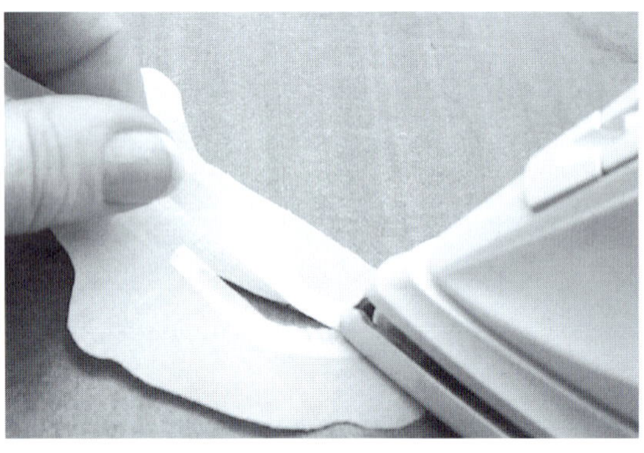

7. Iron the fusible strip to the rim of the eye hole on the wrong side. Remove backing paper.

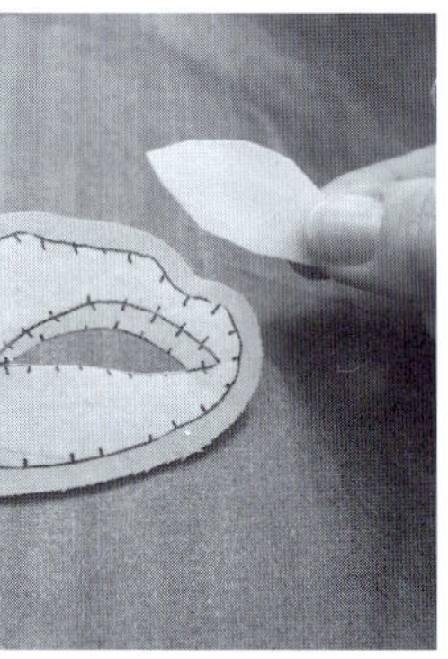

8. Cut 'white of eye' fabric (which may not be white) ...to eye hole size, **plus allowance**, it does not need to be accurately cut to shape. (It is not necessary to use the paper template for this... just make sure that the white of eye fabric is bigger than the hole space.)
Position it behind the hole ..... iron to bond.

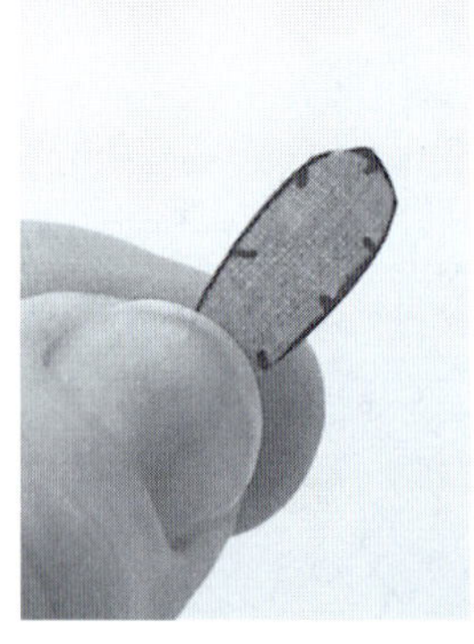

9. Cut iris shape from eye template.
Apply fusible to iris fabric ...
iron the freezer paper iris shape to fabric , cut out with no fabric allowance.

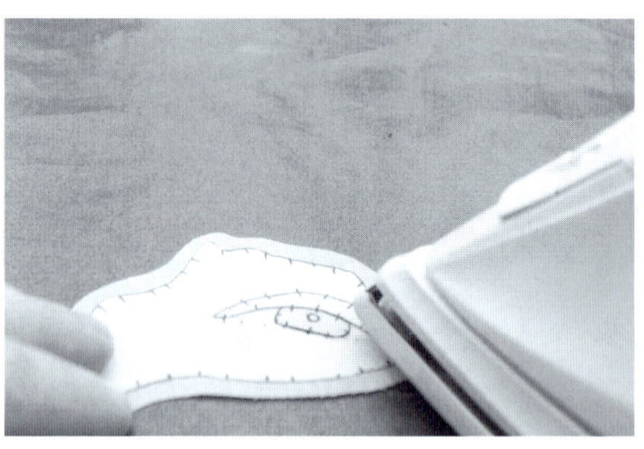

12 Position iris correctly on eye white fabric ... if there is any doubt as to correct position iron white of eye freezer paper shapes in place as guide. Iron iris to bond.
(Adding the highlight follows on page 70).

'Auntie Barbara'
16½ x 19½ ins.
By
Margaret Bright
Chesham, Bucks.

and
Sue Martin.

'Saxon'

30 x 26 ins.

by

Sue Martin.

'Bella'

21 x 16½ ins

By

Mary Rich.

**Harpenden,
Herts.**

'Adam'

15 x 15 ins.

By

Shirley Winchester.

**Harpenden,
Herts.**

"Mono Lake"

23 1/2 x 18 1/2 ins.

by

Alison King.

St. Albans.
Herts.

Fabric images of all kinds can be created using the previous techniques.

The assembly rules are few and very simple to remember....

1. Large and medium shapes have fusible applied to the edges only.

2. Small shapes have fusible applied to the whole of the wrong side.

3. Dark fabric shapes go on top of light.

4. Leave the freezer paper in place until the image is complete ....

Tip !

If you remove a paper too soon you will lose a vital edge for matching neighbouring shapes.

If this should happen ... do not panic ... (this is a kind technique!)
....just re-trace,
re-cut
and re-apply
a duplicate shape in scrap freezer paper !

Crisis over .... relax!!

But ... if like me you are curious....

.... and you get sorely tempted to have a peek ......
remove a paper shape to have a look .. then replace it.

Remove the paper permanently only when you are ***completely*** sure everything due to be fused to that shape is already in place.

5. Trim the outside edge of the subject's silhouette to the paper's edge and always iron strips of fusible web all round the whole image on the wrong side to prevent fraying and in readiness for bonding it to the background.

Removing freezer paper.

Freezer paper is easy to peel away from fabric most of the time. However, during the assembly process, papers will have been ironed many times as edges are fused together and this may have increased the strength of the bond.

Here are a few tips to help with the removal of stubborn pieces of paper.

1. Use the tip of the scissors, or 'quick unpick' to poke under the edge of a paper shape and loosen the bond throughout the shape by sliding it back and forth.

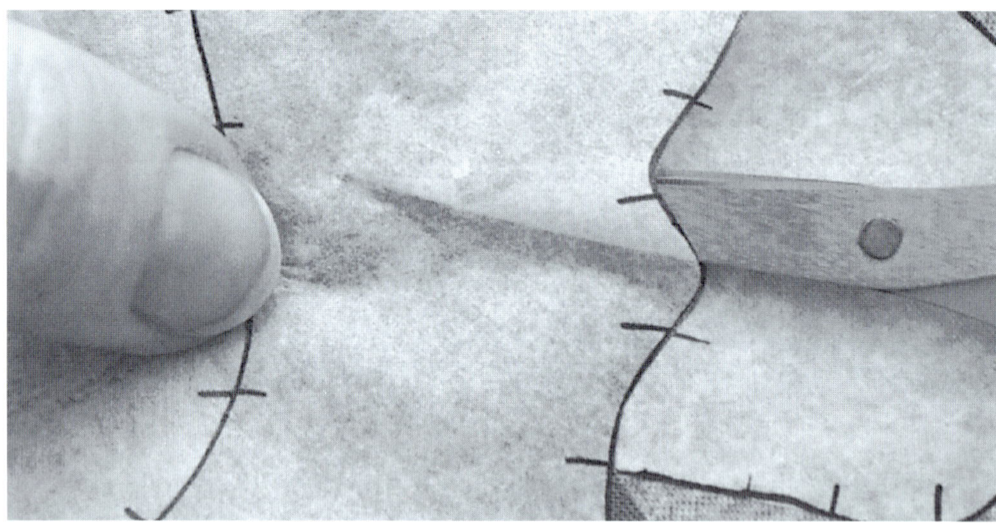

2. If the edge of a paper is accidentally bonded under the fabric of a neighbouring shape .... *do not pull to release.* Trim the paper back to the fabric at the trapped edge .... the small amount left behind under the fabric will not be detectable.

3. If small pieces of paper are left behind on the fabric ... moisten them with a damp cotton wool bud and lightly scratch them with the scissor blade to remove.

4. If most of paper lifts away leaving behind small slivers of the shiny layer .... iron a piece of scrap fabric on top of the work. There is a good chance that the bits of paper will adhere to the scrap fabric and be removed with it.

5. If it is hard to lift the edge of a paper ... do not risk causing the fabric edge to become frayed by continued efforts. Gently pierce the main body of the paper (taking care not to damage the fabric) and work towards the edges as per point 1.

Adding detail.

Now that all the shapes are bonded together and the image is complete, this is the right time to add any further tiny details which are required by permanent pen.

This should always be done before the image is sewn together in case a mistake is made. It is still possible at this stage to separate the fused joins and replace a damaged shape. However, once the joins have been sewn this can no longer happen.

A very light touch is vital when using a permanent pen on fabric ...
Once added, marks cannot be removed.
Practice on paper before marking the appliquéd fabric.

Details will blend in and be softer if added in a series of tiny dots ... therefore a pen with a very fine tip is essential.

Never draw lines ..... always dot !

The most common places to require added detail are ......

Eyes .... adding shading ...... eyelashes .... and pupils.

Noses ... shading ... and nostrils.

Mouths and teeth .... adding shading to lips and between teeth.

Hair ... eyebrows ..... moustaches ... and beards, especially stubble.

The application of dots can also soften hard edges.

Careful scrutiny of both the original photograph and the enlarged photocopy can help clarify where dots are required.

Tip !

The use of a light box to illuminate the fabric image aligned on top of the master design drawing can also be a great help with correctly positioning shading dots.

Bringing eyes to life.

There is little point in risking insanity by trying to appliqué such minuscule circles as the pupils in eyes. Inking them in with a black permanent pen after the eye has been assembled is much easier and just as effective.

The circle can be drawn small and gradually enlarged until it looks right.

With the pupil in place the eye now requires the white spot of reflected light to add sparkle. There may be more than one highlight in a subject's eye. Examine your photo to establish the number, shape and exact position.

Highlights are added by bonding small pieces of fusible mending/binding tape. If the highlights fall within the pupil, cut them slightly larger than required and of approximate shape. Iron the tiny piece of tape to bond it in the right place. Do not assume that this is always centrally placed in the pupil ... once again your photo will guide you as to the exact position. (The tiny pieces of tape can be easily picked up and placed with a wet scissor point).

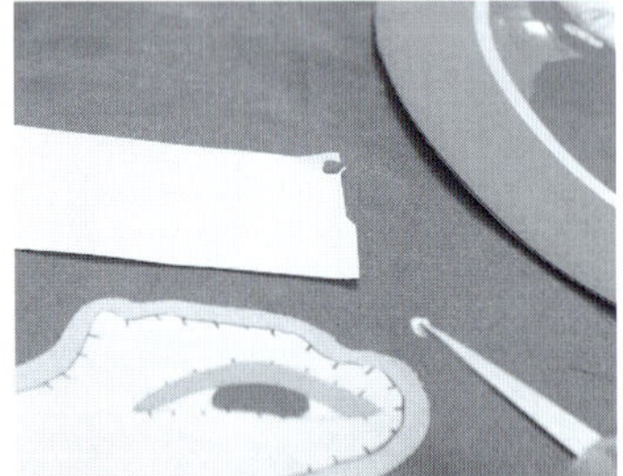

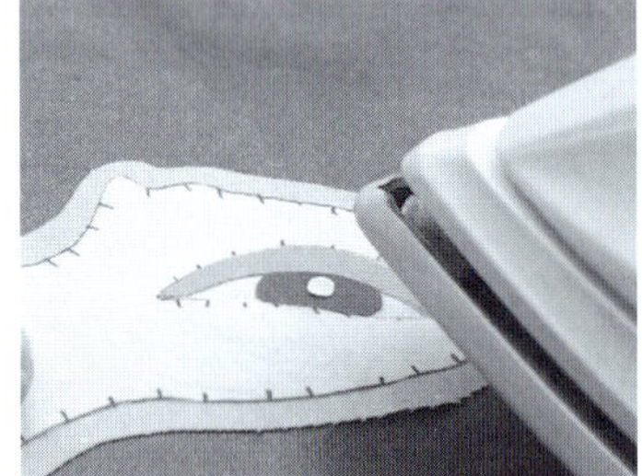

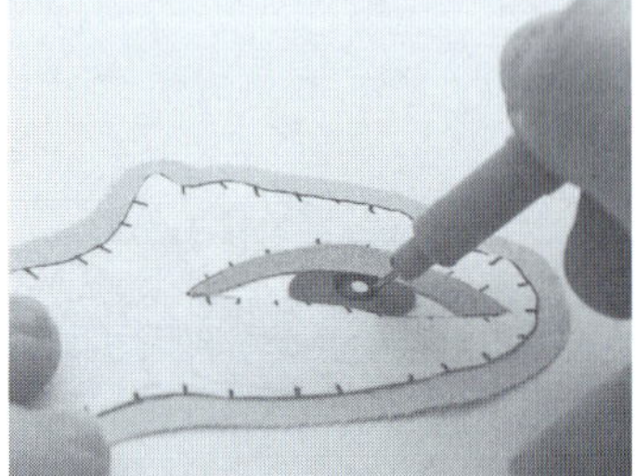

The black pen can be used once again to alter the shape and size of the highlight to correspond with the photographic image. Colouring over the raw edge of the mending tape will disguise it.

If the highlight falls on the iris, cutting it at the right size and the right shape becomes more important, as it is harder to disguise the edge of the tape without a permanent pen to match the iris colour.

The difference that highlights make to eyes is amazing. They are the factor which control the direction in which the eyes appear to be looking.

Where the subject is looking straight ahead, they can make the eyes appear to follow you all round the room and an inanimate fabric appliqué portrait comes to life !

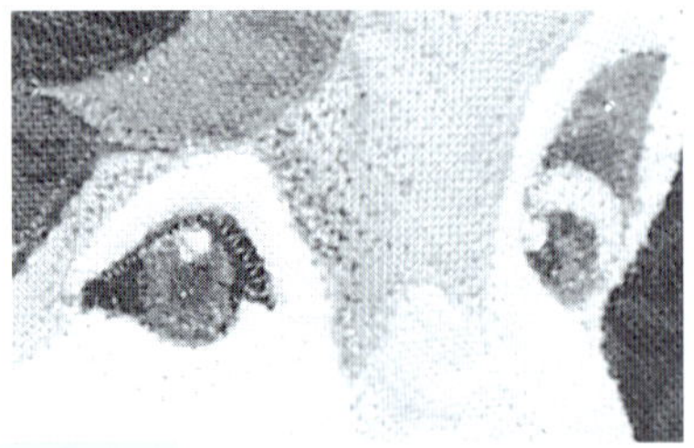

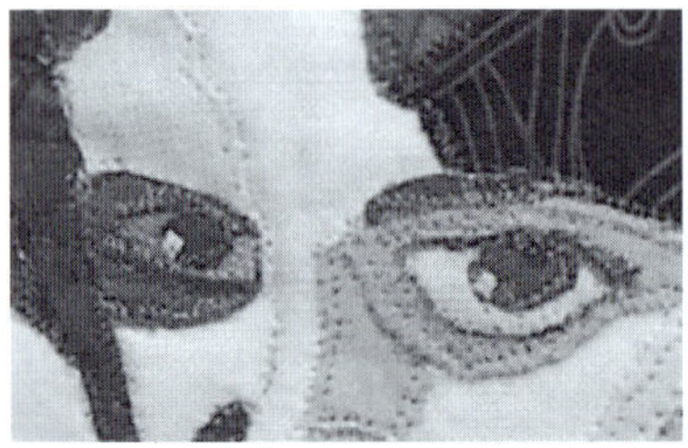

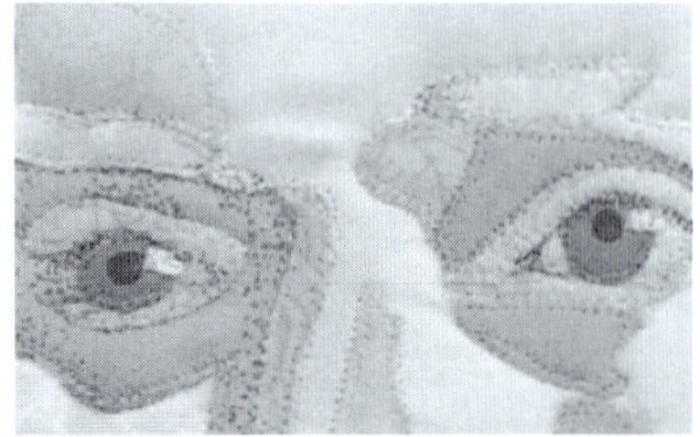

‘ Dad’

23 1/2 x 27 ins.

By
the Author.

William Murphy.
1897-1977

'Washing Day

33½ x 29½ ins.

By

Sue Martin.

Sewing joins.

The sewing stage of these appliqués is really the easiest part of all. Every bonded join needs to be top stitched from the right side of the work to hold the shapes securely together. One possibility would be to use satin stitch. However, that would create a solid line of colour between shapes, harden edges and require many different coloured threads to complete the work.
A better option is to make joins as invisible as possible .... so that they are secure, but affecting the final appearance of the image as little as possible.

Six things are required for successful sewing ......

1. Nylon/Monofilament ...'invisible thread' ...... use ordinary thread in the bobbin. Use 'clear' or 'smoke' to match light or dark fabric.

2. Size 60 machine needles.

3. A well maintained machine, (clean, oil, and check the tension regularly.)

4. A very narrow stitch width setting .... approx. machine setting 1·5.

5. A very short stitch length ... approx. machine setting 1·0.

6. An open toe machine embroidery foot .... which allows an unrestricted view of the area of fabric the needle is about to sew.

The only skill required for success is the ability to zig -zag accurately following a meandering line. This can be quickly perfected with a little practice. The presser foot will need to be lifted at intervals to enable the work to be turned, so that corners and curves can be negotiated. A machine 'knee lift' lever makes this very easy.
The stitching should accurately follow each join, falling almost totally on the **top fabric.** The outer edge of the zig-zag should just clear the far side of the join ... stitching into the lower fabric and completely enclosing the raw edge to seal it.

Take care not to stitch **into** the raw edge itself, as this may cause it to fray and become fluffy. If any stray threads peep out from this edge it is easier to trim them from the fused edge before sewing. Always check the stitching closely and adjust the machine settings as necessary, to give the neatest appearance.
The fine needle will create small holes ...... the thread will be transparent and the result will be as near invisible as possible, and consequently impossible to remove.

However, all mistakes are equally invisible ... (just re-stitch correctly).

Appliquéing the image to the background.

Once the appliquéd image has been stitched, the next consideration is the choice of background.
Below are several options ......

1. There may not be a ***separate*** background at all .... the image may be part of a bigger picture in which whatever is behind it will also have been traced as shapes and continue to be joined in the way described previously.

2.. The image could be applied to a patchwork background. This should be constructed separately using any chosen technique ... and made large enough to include a seam allowance behind the appliqué image.

3. The image could be applied to a single piece of fabric ....
with, or without an added border .... e.g. for a wallhanging.

4. The image could be applied to a single piece of fabric creating a block to be included in a sampler quilt, or used as a central quilt medallion.

5. The image could be applied to a wearable item ....
perhaps the front of a waistcoat or the back of a jacket.

6. A picture mount and fabric frame could be added .... simple or ornate, turning it very definitely into a 'picture' (a favoured option of mine !).

Whatever the choice .... the construction method is the same ....

1. Having applied Bondaweb ™ all round the subject, on wrong side of the trimmed edge, the completed appliqué is ironed to the background fabric, bonding it in place ready for invisible stitching.

2. Stitch all around the outline of the subject first, joining it to the background, using the same small open zig zag.

3. Turn the work to the wrong side and cut away the background fabric behind the appliqué, to within 1/4 in. of the outline stitching. The avoidance of double layers of fabric at this stage will ensure that the work will quilt evenly later on.

4. Check very carefully that all joins throughout the work have been stitched ... it is very easy to miss one or two. Always look at the back of the work when doing this as the stitching, or lack of it, will often show up more clearly there.

“Granny and Nick in ‘The Quilt Store Inc.’

36 1/2 x 29 ins.

by Jenny Hipperson.

"6FX56142"
Circa 1942.
25 x 20 1/2 ins.
By
Nora Field.

Boxmoor.
Herts.

'Victoria'

16 1/2 x 20 ins.

By
Carmen Redler.

Boxmoor.
Herts.

Designing original frames.

This is easy to do and allows choice of style and size. These frames fall into two categories ....

1. Square and rectangular frames
2. Round and oval frames.

Square and rectangular frames.

These are constructed from one single, ... or several joined strips of fabric, which border the top, bottom and sides of the item. The length of these will correspond to the size of the picture they are intended to frame .... the length of the side of the picture .... (**plus,** if mitres are planned ... twice the width of the border and a little extra).

The borders are individually sewn to all four sides of the picture and the corners neatly mitred creating a modern streamlined look.

The same principle applies to frames with a greater number of sides .... e.g. a hexagon.

A more formal traditionally styled frame can be made by appliquéing decorative corners and side additions to the borders.

If you look carefully at the example on the right you will see four corner decorative appliqués .....
and also four side appliqués ....
all of which have been mounted on frame sides made from sewn fabric strips.

Instructions follow and patterns for these shapes begin on on page 92.

Decorative shapes for frames.

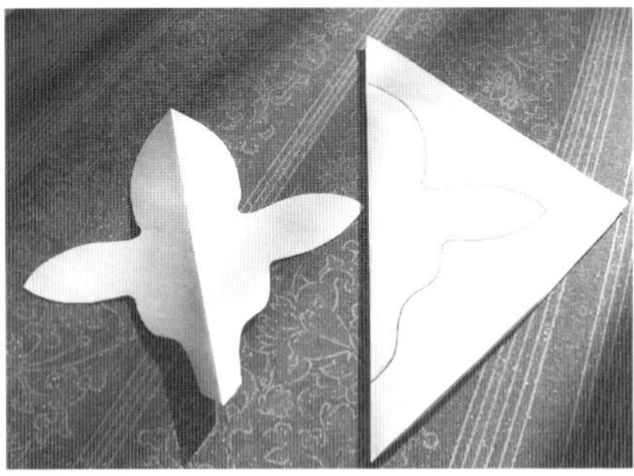

These will be completed in fabric and appliquéd over the side strips which form the frame.

1. Corners are designed on squares or rectangles of freezer paper which are folded diagonally, or vertically in half. Experiment with different sizes and proportions.

2. Begin cutting the paper at the fold ... and continue around the shape, returning to the fold ... creating different shapes.
(If you do not intend to join the corners of frame sides lying under these shapes, make sure that the shapes you have cut will be large enough to completely cover the area which is missing .... with sufficient overlap to allow the edges to be bonded in place).

3. Additional shapes can be drawn on one half of the folded corner and traced through to the other. These can be self contained shapes in each triangle ... or half shapes, if originating and ending on the fold.
A mirror placed along the fold can help you to plan as you go. Shading these shapes in different tones will give them 3D form.

4. Side shapes are designed in the same way using a rectangle of paper. (The same shape can be used in both corner and side positions.)

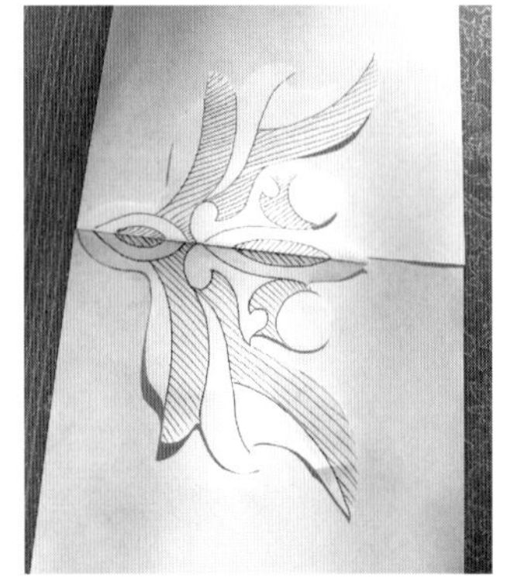

Construction methods are as previously described.
The completed corners (and sides) are appliquéd in position on top of the frame sides. After the decorative shapes have been stitched in place, any frame fabric lying underneath should be cut away .... trimmed to within 1/4 in. of the stitching. Quilts on pages 63, 79 & 80 use similar decorative shapes.

"Grandma Murphy"
31 x 32 ins.

By
the Author.

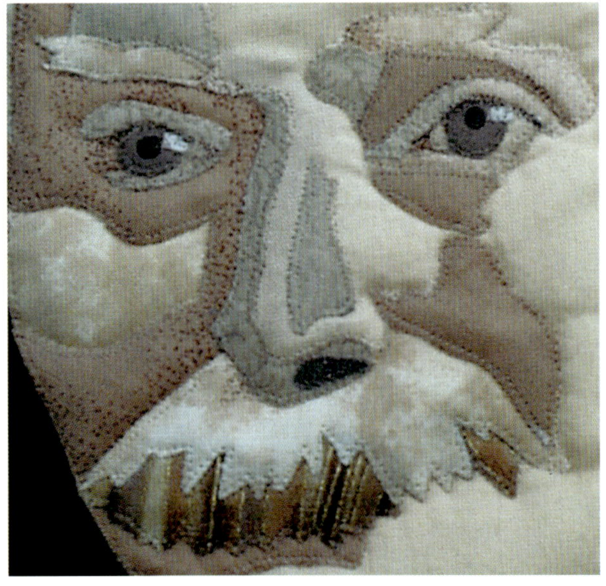

"Grandpa Murphy"

40 x 40 ins.

by
the Author.

Drafting round and oval frames.

Circles.

Large circles for round frames can be drawn on freezer paper by using either ....

1. A large compass
2. A pencil anchored to a central tack with a length of string.

Draw the outer rim, then the inner .... creating the desired frame width between the two.

Ovals

The use of an oval as a frame, or as a 'photo mount' inside a rectangular frame, can be stunning. However, an oval is often thought of as a a more difficult shape to draw.

Here is an easy technique which will enable ovals of any size or proportion ... short and fat ...... tall and skinny .... to be drafted with ease.

1. Decide on the height and the width measurement of the oval you require. These measurements will change the proportions of the oval, and depend upon the size of the picture it surrounds. Fold a sheet of freezer paper which is big enough to accomodate the oval into quarters ... crease the folds flat.

2. Draw two lines at your chosen measurements

The lines should cross each other .... at right angles at their mid points.

3. Label the ends of the longest line .... A and B,
and the ends of the shorter line .... C and D.
Label the point where the lines cross .... O.

4 Cut a strip of paper ....
a little longer than AO ......

5. Mark points .... E F = C O
E G = A O
on the edge of the paper strip.

5. Taking the paper strip place point F on line AO ... and rotate the strip ..... until G touches the OD line.
Mark the freezer paper at point E with a dot ..... this will begin to mark the perimeter of the oval.

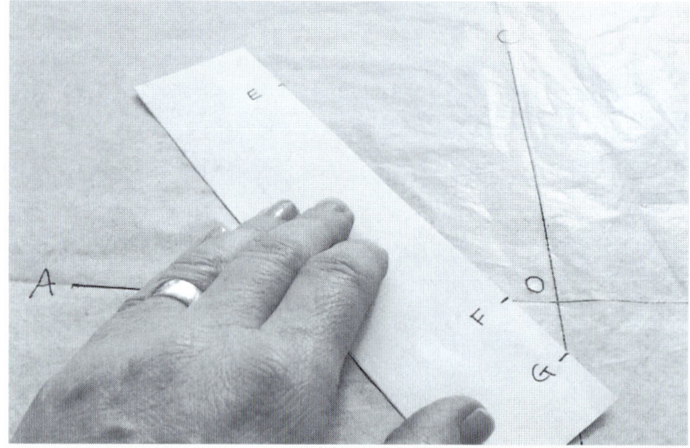

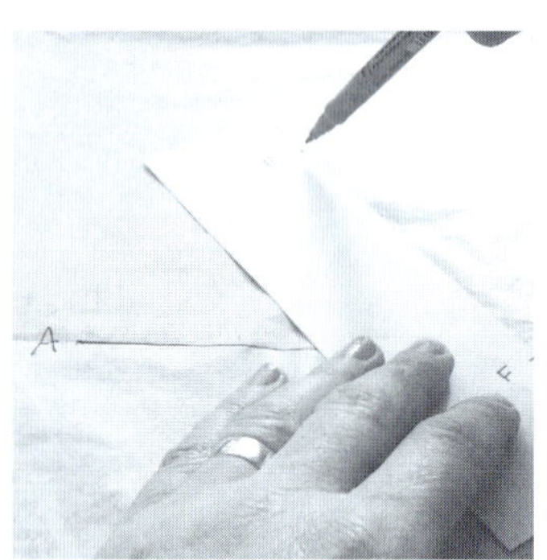

6. Place point F in a new position on line AO ... still placing G on line OD. This will move point E to a new position ..... which should be marked once again with another dot.

7. Continue re-positioning points F and G .... and marking point E until the dots form a clear curve..

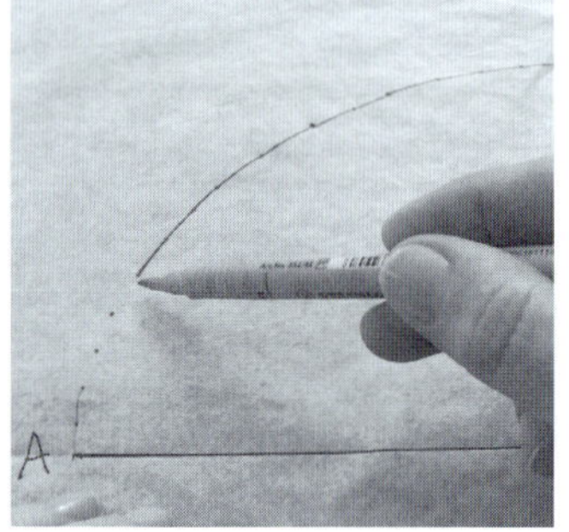

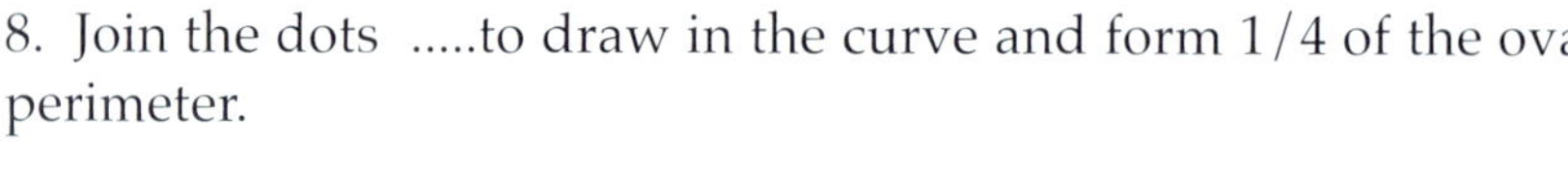

8. Join the dots .....to draw in the curve and form 1/4 of the oval perimeter.

9. Refold the paper into quarters .....
along lines AB and CD ....
keeping the marked curved line in sight.

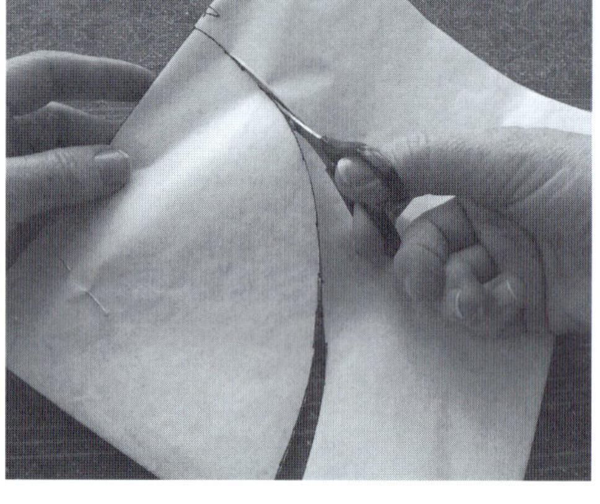

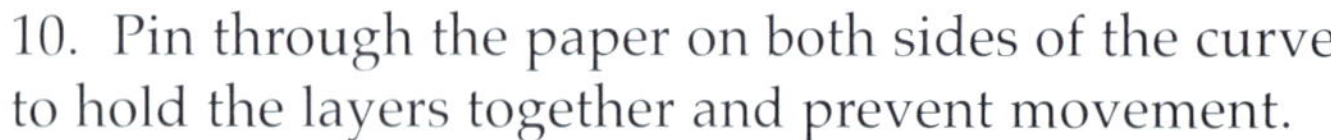

10. Pin through the paper on both sides of the curve to hold the layers together and prevent movement.

11. Cut accurately through all layers along the curved line to create a perfect oval when the paper is unfolded

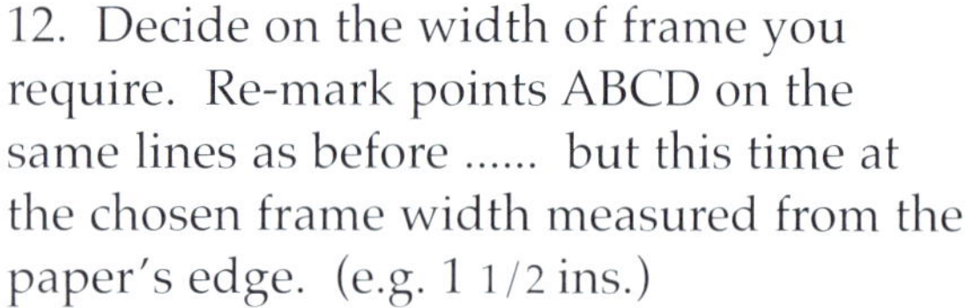

12. Decide on the width of frame you require. Re-mark points ABCD on the same lines as before ...... but this time at the chosen frame width measured from the paper's edge. (e.g. 1 1/2 ins.)

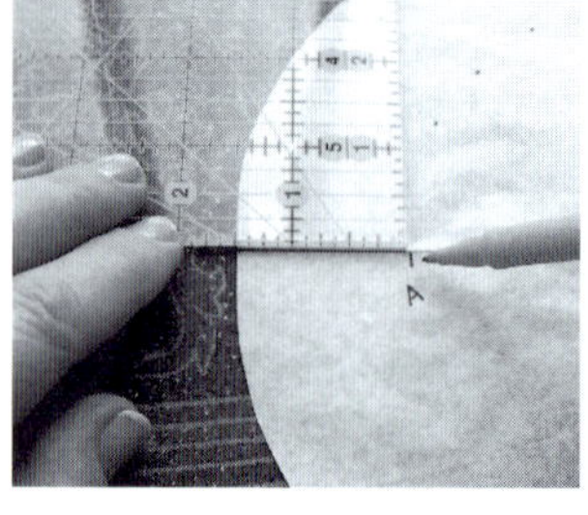

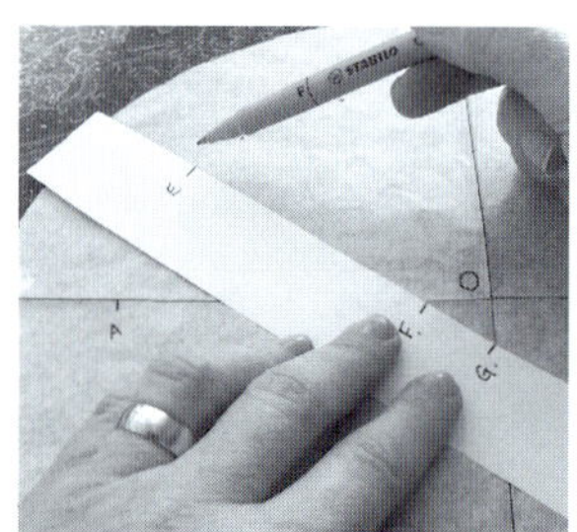

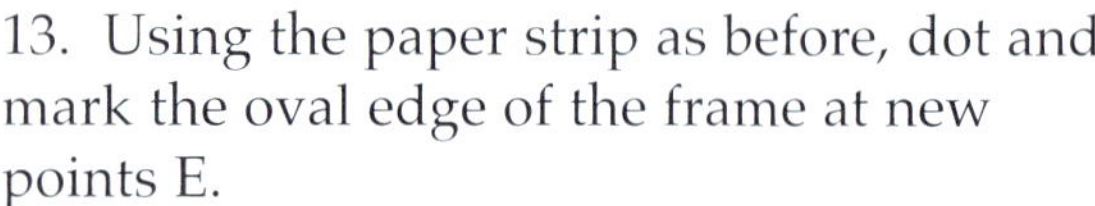

13. Using the paper strip as before, dot and mark the oval edge of the frame at new points E.

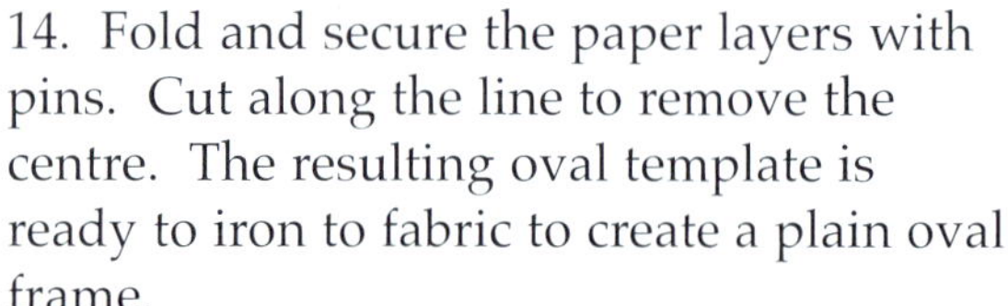

14. Fold and secure the paper layers with pins. Cut along the line to remove the centre. The resulting oval template is ready to iron to fabric to create a plain oval frame.

'Simplicity and Style.
22 ins x 26 ins.

By
the Author

"Come into the garden Maude"

20 1/2 x 25 ins.

By
Sue Martin.

Creating 3D illusion in frames.

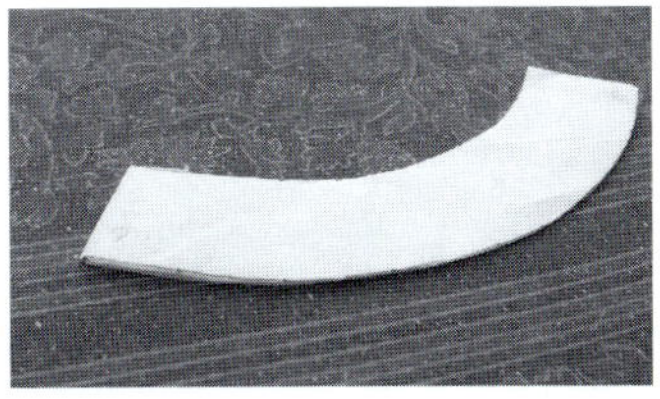

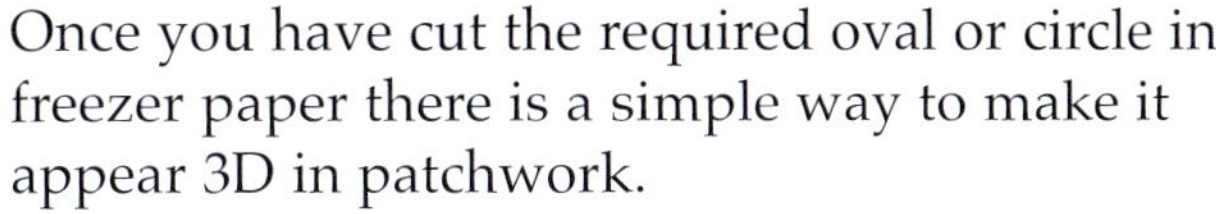

Once you have cut the required oval or circle in freezer paper there is a simple way to make it appear 3D in patchwork.

1. Fold the shape in half, flattening it and matching the folds on the ***inside*** edge very accurately.

2. Repeat, once again matching the folds on the inside edge. Do not worry about the folds on the outside edge.

3. Continue folding until you reach the size of unit that you wish to use.

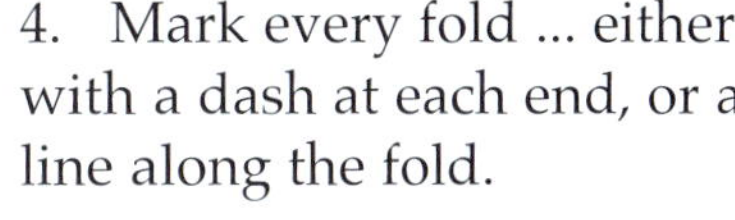

4. Mark every fold ... either with a dash at each end, or a line along the fold.

5. Mark diagonal lines between neighbouring folds .....
alternately from the inside edge out and the outside edge in.

6. Number each section consecutively.

7. Cut each section apart... iron them to the choisen fabric .

8. Cut fabric with 1/4 in seam allowance.

9. Sew together matching fabric right sides and using the edge of the freezer paper as the sewing guide.
(The frame of 'Come into the garden Maude on facing page was assembled using this method.)

10. Experiment by marking extra lines to make the frame design more complex.

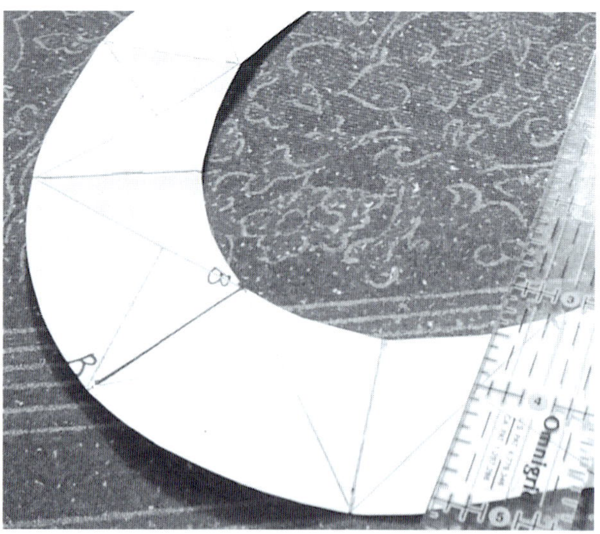

10. If you lay the creased shape on a flat surface it will help to clarify which shapes are dark medium and light. Reproducing these tones in fabric will give your frame a 3D appearance.

If you wish, you can match or contrast the direction of the light source to the photo image.

Below is the lampshade which inspired this idea. The arrangement of the different tones on the pleated paper clearly demonstrates the effect of light.

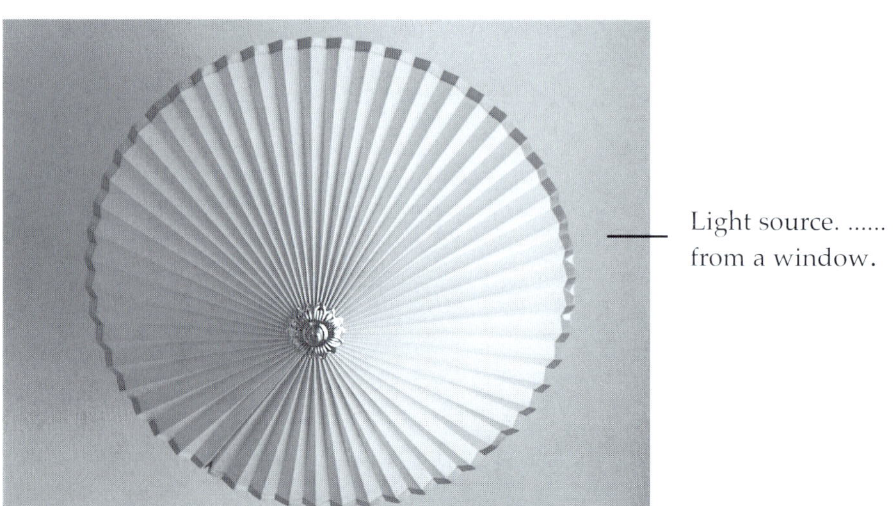

Light source. ......
from a window.

Another type of oval frame can be constructed by drawing curves on the freezer paper oval dividing the frame into separate sections. The frame can be assembled using different fabrics in each section joined together using the fusible appliqué method already described.

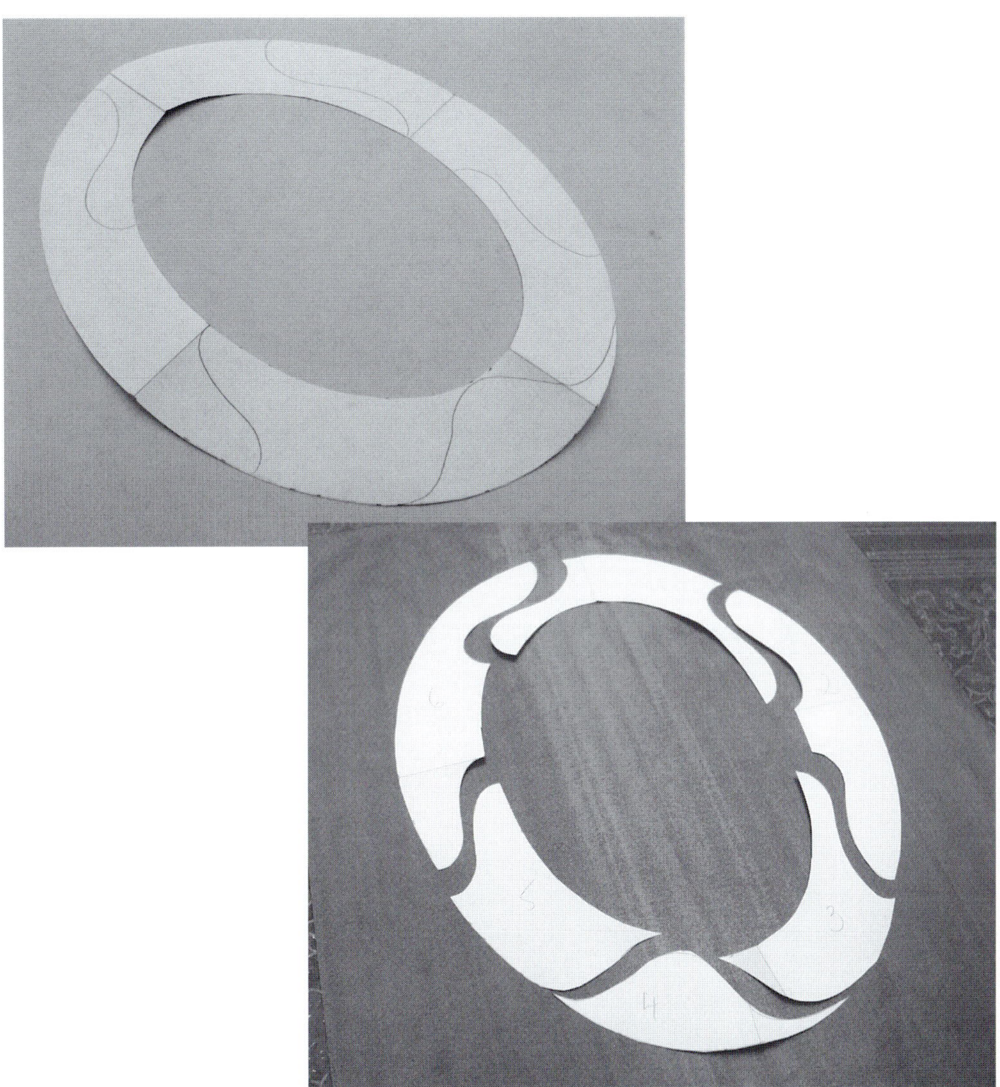

The oval wallhanging 'Dad' on page 71 demonstrates a frame constructed by this method. The fabric colours are relatively close in tone so the separate sections are not noticeable from a distance. (I like a quilt to keep a 'secret' or two for close inspection.) The quilting lines on the frame follow the curves and add interest by creating a different pattern in each section.

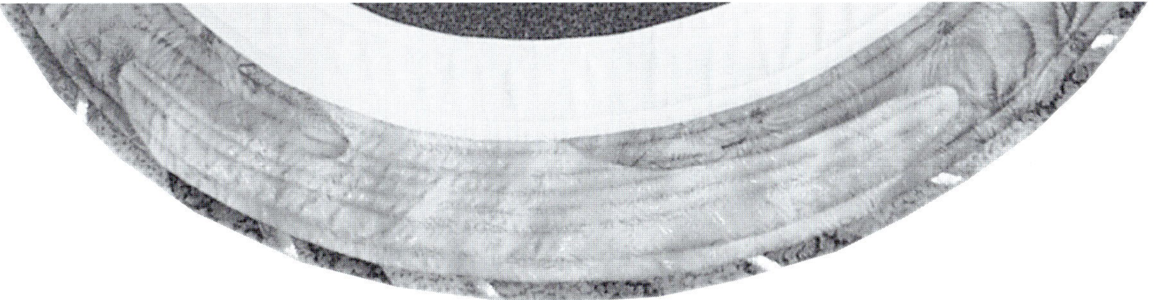

Quilting

Quilting a design is really adding the icing to the cake. Appliqués come to life when three dimensional texture is added.

However, quilting an image which includes a face, or faces, can be daunting. There can be a fear of spoiling the item at the last stage ....
Do not worry .... you will only be adding the dimensional effect ... remember that the actual stitching will be almost invisible.

The following points are worth considering .....

1. Always quilt faces with invisible thread. It is much less intrusive than coloured threads. Coloured and decorative threads can always be used in other parts of the work ... e.g. metallic threads look great on frames.

2. Loosen the top tension of your machine slightly ... it will discourage the bobbin thread from peeping through on the top.
Tightening the bobbin tension slightly will also help.

3. If the background is closely quilted the face will become raised by comparison, and this will enhance the 3D effect.

4. Use the outline of the fabric shapes as the quilting guideline.
You need not quilt around **every** fabric shape ... but leaving large areas of a face unquilted can lead to the subject looking like a victim of 'mumps.
Unquilted areas will also be more likely to become wrinkled during storage and transportation. The odd wrinkle will not disfigure a geometric patterned quilt ... but wrinkles can age, or create a worried look on fabric faces.
Quilt 'in the ditch' just outside the invisible zig zag stitching around **most** if not all shapes. (I usually quilt around all joins.)

5. If you should notice an unstitched join ...... (one that you missed when zig-zagging the shapes together) ...whilst quilting .... **do not panic** ..... **it happens** .... set the machine stitch to the same short zig zag as you used to join shapes and stitch along the join.
This action will anchor the fabric shapes and quilt at the same time ... and only be noticeable if the back of the work is very closely inspected. Once the join has been secured, revert to quilting as before.

6. Quilting needs to be accurately executed to look good. Accurate quilting takes practice ... practice leads to confidence .... confidence brings enjoyment. A short practice period every day will bring improvement faster than several hours every six months.

7. Do not 'give up' on the quilting too soon ... many fair quilts could be good... and many good quilts could be great ... with the addition of a little more quilting.

8. Change the machine needle frequently ... a sharp needle sews more efficiently. Dull needles miss stitches which can spoil the finished effect.

9. Quilting is generally easier to do smoothly if your machine runs at a faster, rather than slower speed. Stitching can get jerky at slower speeds.
(However, metallic threads need a slightly slower pace to discourage them from shredding as you sew).

10. Consider using an automatic machine decorative stitch to quilt parts of a background or frame.

11. A traced working design can also be used as a quilting pattern.
Carbon trace the design onto thin paper, (tracing or greaseproof paper are fine) as they will allow you to see exactly where you are positioning the image.
Pin the paper to your quilt and sew straight through both paper and quilt to save having to mark the fabric.
The perforated paper will pull away when you have finished.

(This also works for accurately positioning quilted facial wrinkles and guide lines for embroidering spectacles or jewellery.

12. Quilts with straight edges can be bound using straight cut strips of fabric.
However, if the edges of a quilt incorporate curves they will require binding with fabric strips which have been cut on the bias.
My favourite way to do this is to sew several different coloured fabric strips together, and then rotary cut across them at 45° producing diagonal stripes throughout the binding.

The gold stripe was added by appliquíng 'Quick Bias' before the diagonal cuts were made.

(The quilts 'Dad'on page 71 and 'Grandma Murphy'page 79 were both bound by this method.)

Labelling your quilt..

If, like me, you choose to use personal photos for your project, the label on the back of a quilt can be a great place to record information about the person, people, or places on the front.
This of course is in addition to the usual maker's name address and date.

If your quilt is likely to be exhibited and you are worried about its getting lost or stolen, ... the label can be sewn to the backing fabric before the item is quilted. Once the quilting is complete it will be almost impossible for this label to be removed ... the quilt is effectively labelled for life.

The wording on the label can be embroidered .... handwritten .... typewritten or computer printed. The last three alternatives are easy to accomplish, if freezer paper is ironed to the back of plain fabric to stabilise it. Handwriting can be done using permanent pen to make it washable. Be aware that both typewritten and computer printed wording will run or fade if washed. However, since the main use of the 'Photo Fabrication' technique is probably for wallhangings, they are unlikely to need washing.

Consider recording relevant names ..... and in addition, dates and any information which may be of interest. A duplicate of the photograph which was used, or a montage, can be created by computer scanning, heat transfer to fabric (shops that print 'T' shirts can do this for you) .... or there are photo printing sheets available at quilt shops for use with a domestic iron.

Above, a scanned and computer printed label.

The inclusion of a pocket on the back of the quilt can enable relevant momentos to be safely stored out of sight until they are required.

The personal value of a quilt can be enhanced by the inclusion of meaningful fabrics, either on the front or the back of the quilt. Ties, fabric from clothing, fabric insets from greeting cards etc. can add interest.

Storing and transporting these quilts.

Like so many other quilters I have always stored quilts by folding them with the right side turned inwards to protect from dirt and damage, and taken care to check that the folds do not remain in the same places for long. However, my experience with 'Photo Fabrication' quilts has led me to change my habits as they require a little extra care during transportation and storage.

Patterns of all kinds can cope with a few wrinkles here and there without the overall appearance being adversely affected. This however, cannot be said for faces ! ..... as soon as a wrinkle appears it suggests worry or ageing and is not an asset. Once formed it may be a nuisance to remove.
It is altogether better to work at preventing their formation in the first place.
The solution is quite simple ....

Store or transport all 'Photo Fabrication' quilts either ....

a. Flat ... supported, but with nothing lying on top of them .....or ....

b. Rolled around a wide girth cardboard tube *with the right side of the quilt turned outwards*. The curve of the tube will cause any wrinkles that develop to be formed on the back of the quilt where they matter least.

Should the odd wrinkle appear it can usually be eliminated by rolling the quilt as described in b. and gently steaming the wrinkle with an iron. Leave the steamed part exposed to the air to facilitate drying ... but at the same time keep the wrinkle stretched over the curve of the roll so that it is discouraged from returning. A little spray starch will also help to prevent this.

(Oh that my own facial wrinkles were as easy to remove !!!)

Frame patterns to copy.

Top section of decorative corner.

1. Trace this half design onto the dull side of folded freezer paper.
(min. size 15 x 16 ins. = 38 x 41 cm.) .... complete the design by adding the traced matching lower section on next page.

2. Trace the half design through to the other side of the folded paper to complete.

3. To duplicate the other three corners take three additional pieces of freezer paper of the same size, stack them underneath first ... dull side up ....
paper clip together ...'sew' around all design lines through all papers, using the machine with no thread in the needle.

4. Label sections with colour choice.

5. Cut apart, iron to fabric and appliqué as described in the text.

6. Position and appliqué to frame in chosen position.

Frame patterns to copy.

Lower section of decorative corner.

Frame pattern to copy.

side decoration.

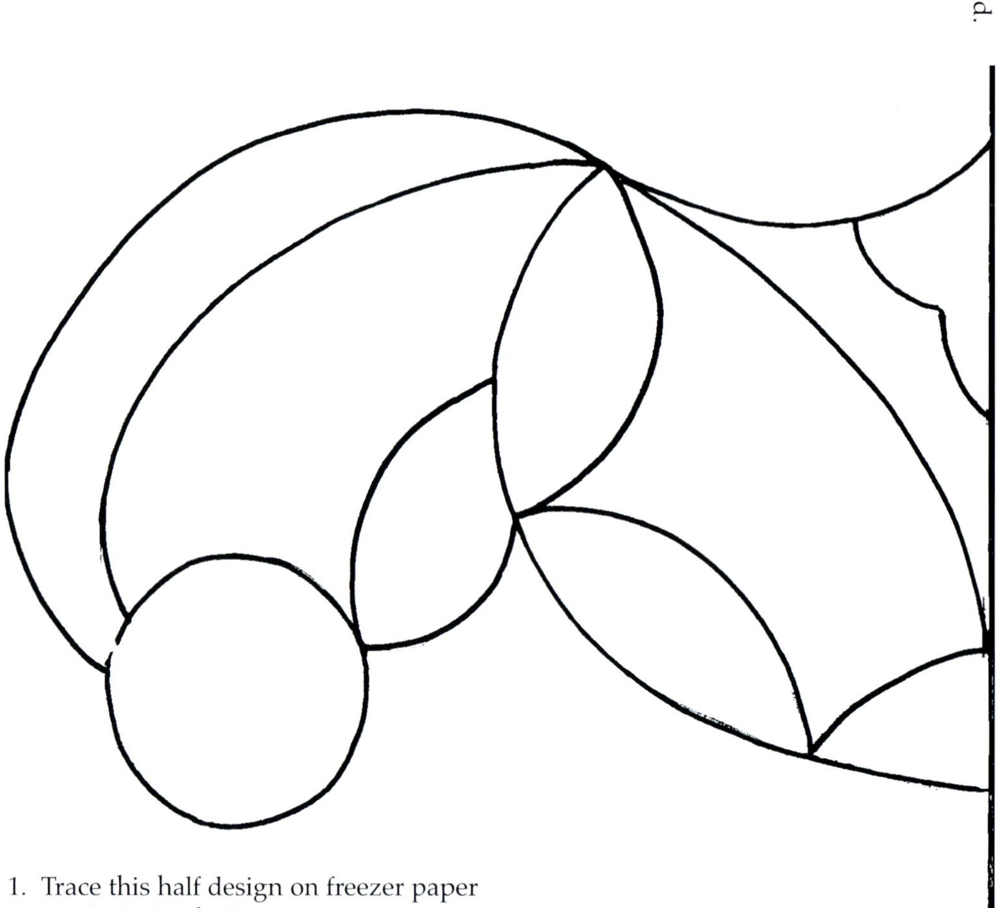

1. Trace this half design on freezer paper .... folded in half.

2. Complete design by tracing the second half on the other side of the folded paper.

3. Label sections with chosen colours.

4. Cut sections apart...iron to fabric and assemble as described in the text.

I do hope that you have enjoyed the quilts in this book ... but perhaps I have an even greater hope that you will be encouraged to have a go and try the technique described.

I also have a fear ... that the great results achieved by those who kindly contributed their work to be photographed ... all of whom were genuinely trying this technique for the first time .... will frighten the less confident sewer. For this reason I would like to finish with a few words of encouragement to anyone wondering if they could make a 'Photo Fabrication.'

The artist Rosetti offered good advice to those daunted at 'the ever receding nature of excellence',

"Dare to be bad .... it is the way forward"

So give it a try ..... get out the family album .... below are some of the photos that we used, and discover just how easy it can be to turn your family photo into your family heirloom !.

Other books and tools by Angela Madden ....

'Sew Easy Celtic'..... A unique easy way to design your own original Celtic knotwork patterns for needlework and other crafts. Absolutely no artistic or mathematical skill needed for brilliant, fast, machine sewn results. Based on drawing symmetrical doodles ....
so anyone can do it ! If you've ever cut out a paper snowflake you can do this!

'Magic Celtic'... More easy designing ... this time using the 'Circle Slice ruler' to draft accurate wedge shaped slices, and more doodles, to create multi-sectional knotwork designs .... they look amazingly complicated ... but are easy to draft and fast to machine sew.

'Applique and Roses'..... An appliqué block and border design technique. This book shows how to easily create limitless original patterns. Fast machine sewing. The same principles can be applied to drafting vine designs also ..... with a new, fast multiple production system for adding 3D roses and leaves. Forget copying other peoples patterns ... be original ..... create your own in half the time!

'Slice up a Circle' ...... easy " geometricks" for patchworkers create wonderful original star, compass, and kaleidoscopic designs. Use the 'Circle Slice ruler' again for easy accuracy.
With freezer paper everything fits together like a jig-saw puzzle, and it's easy to add curves without any curved seam piecing.

'Pieceful Scenes'..... gives the traditional blocks of your choice a brand new look by linking them with a landscape in a three dimensional illusion. If you can draw a straight line using a pencil and a ruler you already have all the skills required to draft your own original 3D designs. Freezer paper piecing facilitates fast, trouble free assembly.

'Paradise Flowers'..... a unique and easy way to design and machine sew original flower patterns ... traditional style or as 'different' as you choose to make them ... any size for any project. As usual, no artistic ability is required for brilliant results. One pattern on its own looks good ... but assemble them in multiples in different combinations and they look amazing ! Patterns can be used for patchwork, quilting, a new method of 'stained glass' appliqué, stencilling, embroidery or trapunto.

Tools

The 'Circle Slice Ruler'..... takes all the inaccuracy out of drafting precise angles for multi-sectional designing .... none of the problems associated with using a protractor !

The ' Multi - Plait Tool'..... a tool which helps you to draft plaited (braided) designs quickly and accurately in different styles and sizes. These designs are suitable for quilting, embroidery, appliqué or bias appliqué, for both block and borders using varying numbers of cords. It is really easy and speedy to use ...... and it takes plaits correctly around corners for you too !

The 'Feather Tool'.... traditional feathered wreathes, borders, hearts, squares etc. are universally popular designs. This tool is the essential aid to fast, original drafting ... it will feather any shape and in any size for quilting, embroidery, appliqué and bias appliqué.

Video.

'Creative Celtic' ....made in conjunction with Nancy Zieman's U.S. Public T.V.s program host of 'Sewing with Nancy. In this video Angela demonstrates her unique Celtic design techniques and shows many examples of her work.
Video is available by mail order only from ....
Nancy's Notions. 333 Beichl Ave. P.O. Box 683. Beaver Dam, WI 53916-0683. U.S.A.
Credit Card Order Line Tel U.S. 1-800-833-0690. Fax. 1-800-255-8119.